BETSEY FREMANTLE

*TRAVELS IN THE TWO SICILIES*

1817-1820

edited with an introduction and notes

by

NIGEL FOXELL

MAILER PRESS

Mailer Press
50 Comeragh Road
London
W14 9HR

mailerpress@googlemail.com

www.mailerpress.co.uk

Published by Mailer Press, 2007

ISBN 978-0-9553991-0-7

Printed and bound in Great Britain by Cambridge University Press

This book originally appeared in 2001 under the title *Viaggio nelle due Sicilie, 1817-1820*, and was published by Arnaldo Lombardi. Besides Betsey Fremantle's original English, it included an Italian translation, by Nigel Foxell, who wrote the introduction and notes in both languages.

# PREFACE

This publication stems from an encounter at the British Institute of Florence, where I had delivered a lecture on Nelson. During the party that followed it, my friend David Russell, an English painter long domiciled in Florence, took the opportunity of introducing me to Richard Fremantle, the author of *Florentine Gothic Painters* and a descendant of our diarist. It is to him that I owe my contact with his cousin, Commander John Fremantle, now Lord Cottesloe, who inherited the volumes in manuscript from which I have selected the pages that appear between these covers.

At first sight I found Lady Fremantle's handwriting almost illegible: she neither dots her 'i's nor loops her 'e's; here is a pen that travels like Canaletto's brush when he is depicting the waves of the Lagoon; and, submerged by these, I felt at times in great danger of drowning.

One grows acclimatized, however. Only the names presented a real problem, partly because she mis-spells them at times: Wurmbrand, for instance, appears as 'Wolbrann', Consalvi as 'Gonzales', Plasket as 'Plakett'; I have silently corrected them throughout.

I have shortened a number of entries, inserting three dots. Besides the people I have already mentioned, I would like to thank Dr. Emanuele Giliberti, who introduced me to the publishing house of Arnaldo Lombardi, and Mrs. Ilia Warner whose generous advice has been invaluable.

# INTRODUCTION

I am very happy to present this sample from the unpublished diaries of Lady Fremantle. I do not claim that it is more than a tiny offering compared with the entire corpus, or even with what has already been published by the Oxford University Press*. But to my mind she is here at her most illuminating: under the impact of Southern Italy, the enquiring and shrewd mind of this cosmopolitan Englishwoman emerges with unequalled force. The people, the landscape, the arts, all undergo her scrutiny. Even the everyday life of visits and opera-going are recorded, and these too I have included or the picture would have been distorted.

Betsey Wynne - to give her her maiden name - was born in 1778 at Falkingham in Lincolnshire, the second of five daughters of a French mother and a father who was half Anglo-Welsh, half Italian. After wanderings around England, in 1787 the family left for the Continent. A couple of years later the eleven-year-old Betsey opened the first of her diaries which she was to write uninterruptedly till her death in 1857. It may well be that this regular activity developed as a salve, furnishing an element of continuity amidst moves of a frequency that seems inexplicable. What were they after, these Wynnes? The one certainty is that from the outbreak of the Revolutionary and Napoleonic Wars this restlessness

* *The Wynne Diaries*, edited by Anne Fremantle, in 3 volumes, 1935, 1937, 1940. In 1952 an abridged edition appeared in 'The World's Classics', and this re-appeared as a paperback in 1982.

became more a matter of flight then quest. At last, on June 24th, 1796, when the blue-white-and-red tricolour had pursued them as far as Tuscany, they embarked in a British frigate. If this was an act of desperation on the part of Mr. Wynne, Betsey was to see it in another light: 'I was quite delighted and regretted no more that the French had obliged us to run away.' Indeed not: the frigate captain who had taken them under his protection was none other than a certain Thomas Fremantle.

Six months later, in the Palazzo Sessa, the Neapolitan residence of Sir William and Lady Hamilton, Betsey became Mrs. Fremantle.

She was eighteen; he was thirty-one. She was rich; he was poor. She was of very mixed blood and domicile; he was purely English. She, like her French mother and her Italian paternal grandmother, was Roman Catholic; he was Anglican.

The marriage was an extremely happy one.

Three days later the newly-weds had re-embarked, and in July they were still at sea for Nelson's catastrophic amphibious action at Tenerife. Here the future national hero, accompanied by Captain Fremantle, was at the point of setting foot on shore when a Spanish bullet struck him in the arm. On account of his concern for Mrs. Fremantle he might have lost his life; but in actual fact she may well have saved it: the wounded admiral found himself in a boat that was crowded with survivors from a sunken cutter, and this was making its way back to the squadron when he heard someone say that the nearest ship, towards which the pilot had been steering, was Captain Fremantle's frigate. Nelson refused to board it. Warned that any further delay would endanger his life, he answered: 'Then I will die; for I would rather suffer death than alarm Mrs. Fremantle by her seeing me in this state, when I can give her no tidings whatever of her husband.' The boat accordingly pressed on till it reached the flagship, where Nelson's arm was immediately amputated. As luck would have it, the surgeon was Monsieur Ronicet, a monarchist refugee of the highest reputation, whereas it transpired that the one in the ship with Betsey on board was disastrous, a veritable disease in his own right. His patients were to include her poor husband, who likewise had an arm wound, though not to the point of requiring amputation.

He suffered even more than Nelson. But in our diarist the two invalids at least had a comforter during the long passage back to England.

Captain Fremantle, still far from being cured - if indeed he ever was - missed the Battle of Aboukir (1798), but he managed to fight at Copenhagen (1801) and Trafalgar (1805). In December, 1806, he returned to England, and was appointed to a seat at the Admiralty.

Meantime he had bought a house at Swanbourne in Buckinghamshire, which, though less than grandiose, accorded with his rank and was adequate for his ever-growing family.

On July 30th, 1810, the captain was promoted admiral. A month later he was appointed to a command in the Mediterranean. In 1811 he went to Sicily as second-in-command to Lord William Bentinck, and in 1812 he was given a squadron in the Adriatic. In 1814 the Austrian Emperor conferred on him the Order of Maria Theresa, the King of England the Order of the Bath, and the King of Naples the Order of St. Ferdinand and Merit. Your average knight can be told by the star on his breast, but Sir Thomas Fremantle was to wear a veritable constellation.

In 1818 he was appointed Commander-in-Chief of the Mediterranean Fleet.

The following year he died in Naples.

For more than a couple of years he had not seen England. On July 25th, 1815, exactly a month after the news of Waterloo had reached Swanbourne, the Fremantles, accompanied now by their children, found themselves once again on the Continent. Landing at St. Malo, they drove across France and Switzerland. In October they reached Italy, where, the Jacobin threat having been finally scotched, they lingered as long as their fancy dictated.

On March 7th, 1817, the Fremantles arrived in Rome, and on April 12th they set out for Naples. Their first stop was Albano. And it is here that we join them.

1817

April 13, Terracina. We left Albano before six o'clock & were made to take six horses the first stage, the road being hilly till after Velletri, when one descends to the Pontine Marshes, through which the road is quite excellent, & the country in the marshes better cultivated than it is in the neighbourhood of Rome. We arrived before three o'clock at Terracina, where we remained, fearing not to get before dark to Mola di Gaeta over the robbing country...

April 14, Naples. We set out from Terracina at six with a couple of dragoons to escort us.[1] Mr. Cornwall, who had all Mrs. Caulfield's diamonds with him, followed us with an escort also to the frontier, only six miles from Terracina. The road is along the sea shore, with steep dreary mountains on the left, & looks frightful, but we saw no *banditti*. On entering the Kingdom of Naples,[2] the Austrians have pickets of eight or ten soldiers every mile all the way to Naples. Fondi is a horrid, dismal place, & the multitude of beggars beyond anything I ever saw. We had bad horses, &, fearing we should get late into Naples, had some dinner at a horrid inn at S. Agata. We only got into Naples at eleven o'clock. I had written to Fanny to get us a lodging. We found no note at the gate, & could not find out the Danvers. We drove to all the inns. They are all full. And had it not been for Mr. Cornwall I think we must have slept in the carriage. He procured for us three rooms near l'Albergo Reale.

April 15. Our little rooms are very comfortless, but have a balcony on Strada Toledo[3] towards the square of the Royal Palace, a very gay, bustling & most noisy scene in the world...

April 16. We removed after breakfast to a very good apartment, but not in a gay situation as it does not look to the sea. But the rooms are clean & nicely fitted up, & look to a terrace with flowers, which is more cheerful than the street. It is 13 Strada Nardone[4], & we are to pay for a month 80 dollars. We have taken an intelligent *laquais de place*, named Raffaello, 8 carlins a day, & a very good carriage & horses for 3 dollars a day. I went to pay some visits, & drove along the sea shore towards Posillipo. Murat[5] has made a beautiful new road, which extends three miles, & was to have met the old road to Pozzuoli, but now remains unfinished. Fremantle[6] dined at the Gunns. I stayed this evening at home. The French Ambassador & the Dsse. de Narbonne call'd, & were most particularly civil to me. It rained tonight, & the weather is really quite cold & unsettled. There was an earthquake last night at eleven o'clock, & it is expected there will be an eruption of Vesuvius: it throws up a great deal of fire.

April 20. ...We had a fine day for our excursion, & walked up to the Solfatara Mountain, formerly a volcano, that is to say 2,000 yrs. ago. It has since only smoked, & is cover'd with sulphur. In the places where holes have been dug there is boiling water. We walked over the crater, which is quite hollow. We then went to see the remains of an amphitheatre, of the Temple of Minerva, & in the town that of Serapis, which is very curious. The marble pavement still remains, & some large & fine columns. We returned by four o'clock & went to dine at the Dsse. de Narbonne's, where we only met the Nugents[7]. The Dsse. gave me her box at S.

Carlo[8]. I went with the girls & was much amused with the ballet of *Giocondo*.

April 23. ...We dined at the English Minister's, Mr A'Court, the party rather formal... Mrs. A'Court is very pretty. We then went to the opera in old Genicco's box, which was quite fill'd up by our party. The opera now closes for a fortnight on account of the Feast of St. Januarius. The miracle takes place on 4th May.

April 25. Felton Hervey[9] was to be married yesterday to Miss Bacon, sister of Jérôme Buonaparte's[10] wife, Mrs. Paterson. I think Mrs. W. Fremantle[11] must be greatly annoyed about it. She is a Roman Catholic...

April 30. Mr. Anderson went with us to the Lago Agnano. The weather was fine, & this small lake stands at the back of the Solfatara Mountain in a retired & pretty situation. It was the effect of an earthquake, which swallow'd up the town of Agnano. The ruins of it may be seen under the lake when the water is very clear[12]. The famous Grotta del Cane is close to the lake. It is very small. A vapour[13] rises from the earth about two feet, which would occasion instant death to anyone breathing it for several minutes. To prove this, a poor dog is laid down at the bottom of the grotto. In a few moments the poisonous air occasioned convulsions. The poor animal foamed at the mouth, & remained quite stiff. On being taken out into the air he soon recover'd. They can only stand this miserably cruel trial eleven times[14]. It kills them after the eleventh...

May 1. We went to a grand review of the Austrian troops in the Champ de Mars. There were 5,000 men. They went through all their manoeuvres & evolutions, & it was a remarkably pretty sight. All the English &

foreigners were there in their carriages, but not one Neapolitan.

May 3. Fremantle went with the minister, Mr. A'Court, to the King[15] at Portici[16] at eleven o'clock this morning. We had a very fine day, & went with the Danvers, Mr. Foley & Mr. Montgomery to see the museum at Portici. All the paintings of the walls found at Pompeii & Herculaneum are kept there. They are very curious, some tolerably well preserved, & most of them in the Arabesque style, like those found in Titus's baths, which served for pattern to Raffaello[17]. Pompeii was destroy'd by earthquake in the yr. 79 of our era, & only discover'd in the yr. 1758. We were shown all the utensils & tools[18] which were found; charcoal, bread, dough, barley, wheat, etc. The skull and arm bone of the woman who was found, her dress was red & gold. The earrings, bracelet & rings are still preserved at the studio at Naples, as also oil, wine, etc. We went down by torchlight, or rather tallow candlelight, into Herculaneum. The amphitheatre is the only thing to be seen, as the best of the excavations have been fill'd up again, & only corridors & low passages remain cover'd with lava. Herculaneum was discover'd by the digging of a well. We return'd to Naples by ½ past four (the road from Portici, about 4 miles, is built up the whole way) & went at five o'clock to the church of Sta. Chiara, where the miracle of St. Januarius[19] was to take place, tomorrow being the feast of this patron saint. The church is very handsome. The middle was kept clear, & inside the railing of the altar all the foreigners had places. The silver image of St Januarius, cover'd with jewels & with a magnificent tiara of jewels on his head, stood on the altar, surrounded by candles. All the old women screamed & yell'd every now & then, imploring the saint. One old woman, who fancies herself related to him, would come up to the altar to

4

exhort him & pray'd out loud[20] to St. Januarius. At last the procession arrived: 39 silver figures of different saints were carried & the blood of St. Januarius, which is kept in a small phial inside the relic, was brought from the cathedral church & placed on the altar. This blood is congeal'd, & the French have never been able to discover by what process the priests get it to liquefy. The Archbishop held the phial in his hand, turn'd it about, the people all in anxious expectation, the old women screaming most horribly. At last, after 35 minutes, the miracle took place, & the blood was shown in a liquid state. The yells increased, & the courier was sent off to announce the happy intelligence to the King, & the priests took the relic into the convent to show it to the nuns, & afterwards carried it back to the cathedral church, where the same miracle is to be performed every morning at ten o'clock for a week. Mr. Cornwall return'd home with us after nine o'clock to dinner.

May 4. We went this evening to a party at the Dsse. de Narbonne's. A lady sang, & afterwards some waltzes & French country dances were danced. I play'd for them.

May 6. We had a lovely day for our excursion to Pompeii... The road is through Portici & Torre del Greco. It is dreadfully dusty, the distance about 14 miles. On our arriving at Pompeii we walk'd entirely over it, & first saw the two small theatres, the temples of Isis, Aesculapius, & then went on to the large amphitheatre, which was only discover'd two years ago, & is now quite clear'd. But all the paintings round the wall of the arena, which were very perfect when first dug out, are now destroy'd. We then went to the Forum, which has also lately been excavated. Some statues & curious things have been found, & a great number of men are still employ'd clearing away the ruins. From this we went to the town of Pompeii, which is very interesting. The streets were narrow & houses small. The marks of wheels are still perceptible on the pavement. Our cicerone told us that it was not lava which cover'd Pompeii, but that an earthquake sunk the houses, & a shower of hot rain & pumice stones, quantities of which are still about, cover'd it. Only seventeen skeletons were found in the cellar of a house outside the town. It is suppos'd they took shelter there. The tombs on each side of the road, just out of the gate, where the urns containing their ashes were kept, are very perfect, & some of them very handsome. Most of the houses were painted inside. Some of the figures still remain, & the pavement was in different colour'd marble, & mosaics. On our return to the square of the ancient barracks, where a shabby set of Neapolitan soldiers now dwell to protect these ruins from being pilfer'd, we had our dinner on a marble table under some weeping willows. We had carried cold meat, pies, & Mr Foley some champagne. We then return'd to Naples, cover'd with dust & rather tir'd with our excursion. Mr. Cornwall drank tea & sat with us in the evening.

May 12. Mr. Cornwall & Mr. Dundas went with me & the girls to Vesuvius. We set out at ½ past three from Naples. At Resina, just beyond Portici, we each mounted a donkey or mule, & began to ascend the mountain, with Salvatore our cicerone at our head, & followed by men & boys carrying our provisions. The road is very easy to the Hermitage, where a few trees still remain, & form a great contrast with the surrounding lava & desolate appearance of the mountain. We got some of the hermit's famous Lacrima Christi wine, & went on. We rode half an hour farther & then were obliged to continue our fatiguing journey on foot. The mountain is so dreadfully steep that it is almost perpendicular, & the ashes so deep that one sinks, half knee-deep, which makes it very fatiguing. With the assistance of a strap which was put round the cicerone's waist & which I held in my hand, he pull'd me up, but the exertion is very great, & the path over irregular sharp pieces of lava very difficult. We had not a clear evening for our excursion: the summit of Vesuvius was cover'd by clouds, & it did not dissipate entirely, but just for an instant I could discern the Bay of Naples. The view of it is beautiful in clear, fine weather. This fog added to the horror of this scene of desolation. On reaching the top we pass'd the cave, where the ground begins to be dreadfully hot, & from the old crater we had a famous view of the volcano, which every ten minutes burst out with a violent explosion, & threw up a quantity of fire & red hot stones, which fell on the ground not far from where we were sitting. I own it look'd very frightful. Just before night closed we walk'd over rocks of lava to the stream of burning lava which was running. We then return'd to our hole fronting the two craters, & ate our dinner by torch light. It is not now safe to go up to the crater; indeed I thought we were quite near enough, & when these eruptions burst out, they lighted all the mountain, & the effect was magnificent. Mr Cornwall sent some chickens to be broiled in the red hot lava; & after dining - I cannot say very heartily, for there was something most awful in these regions of fire, smoke & sulphur - we began to descend by torchlight. One sinks dreadfully deep, & slides down very quickly. I believe it took us not more than a quarter of an hour to return to our mules - we were above an hour climbing. At the Hermitage we again rested, & wrote our names in the book which is kept there, & where very silly remarks, & more silly verses, are written by the travellers of different nations who have visited the mountain. We found our carriages at Resina & arrived at ½ past twelve at Naples, rather fatigued with our excursion, & cover'd with black dust & smoke.

May 13. I felt very tired & very stiff with my Vesuvius excursion...

May 14. Dined a party of twelve at the trattoria on the sea...

May 15. We all went to dine at Ct. Genicco's villa. It was a lovely day, & he gave a most brilliant *fête*. The dinner was to 60 people, one table out of doors, with a band of music playing. We then walked over the grounds, which are in the style of an English shrubbery, & a large orange grove. In the evening we were first entertain'd with the marionettes, then a ventriloquist, & afterwards with a ball. I stayed till one o'clock.

May 16. ... We...went to dine at Ct. Nugent's to meet Lord Temple, who has made up his mind to going to Rome before the malaria comes on. We went in the evening to Fanny, met our usual party & took leave of them all.

May 17, S. Agata. We set out from Naples at five in the morning & have to encounter the misery of a nine days' *voiturier* journey to Florence. We pay only 25 louis; he pays all expenses, excepting the two nights that we remain at Rome. It was very dusty & very hot.
At Capua we rested a couple of hours, & then went on to S. Agata, a wretched bad inn, but the country about it very pretty...

May 18, Terracina. We went in the carriages soon after four, & reached Molo di Gaeta at nine. I went to mass, & afterwards had a comfortable breakfast. The inn is not very bad, upon the sea, & the view of Gaeta & the bay exceedingly pretty. We remain'd two hours, & in six hours' more slow travelling we got into Terracina. The misery of Itri & particularly Fondi is quite distressing. The people are really starving, & some of the poor little children that were carried out to beg seem'd dying for want. I cannot understand what occasions this misery as all the country is cover'd with fine crops of corn, & is exceedingly well cultivated. There are few villages on the hill, & scarcely any on the road, but just the post towns, so that one would suppose there was employment for these poor wretches, but they are all in a state of starvation.

May 19, Velletri. We were away before five, & our *vetturino* trotted across the Pontine Marshes, & did not stop until Torre dei Tre Ponti, 24 miles, where we remained two hours at a horrid inn, full of travellers by *vetturino*, & where the scirocco wind across these marshes made it dreadfully oppressive & unpleasant. But we found it quite suffocating in the carriage, going foot-pace to Velletri. Ld. Temple[21] pass'd us in an open carriage, & complain'd bitterly of the heat. Indeed I never felt anything like it, & think it was owing to the bad air of these Pontine Marshes. We arrived at six o'clock at Velletri, & found the inn very tolerable & the people civil. The Admiral was so overcome by the heat that he could not dine with us, & laid down the moment he arrived. Most of the carriages we met had an escort , but we came without one.

*Before returning to the Kingdom of the Two Sicilies, the Fremantles spent almost a year and three-quarters in Tuscany. Wa rejoin Betsey at Florence.*

## 1819

March 1. I set out from Casa Pucci[22] at seven. The day cleared up & eleven hours' easy travelling brought us to Leghorn, where we found the Admiral, Charles & Stephen[23] at the Villa di Londra. We have a tolerable good apartment, the ship not yet arrived but expected daily...

March 2. The noise from the dockyard made me wake & get up early. The Racer cutter, tender to the flagship, arrived this morning & Lieut. Dawson came on shore in the eveng. He knows nothing of the Rochfort, & saw no more of her since they sailed from Plymouth, but she had left Gibraltar a day before the cutter, & a signal for a man-of-war was made today which is supposed must be the Rochfort.

March 3. We were on the mole all day looking out for the ship, which only came to an anchor after sunset & cannot get pratique[24] till tomorrow...

March 4. I walked to the pratique house as soon as I was dress'd to see Harry[25], who was with Capt. Green, Capt. Noel & Mr. Munroe[26] in the quarantine place, waiting for pratique, which Mr. Falkner after many pompous speeches & unnecessary formalities gave them at eleven o'clock...

March 7. We all dined at the Governor's, Spanocchi... The Admiral, dress'd out in all his orders, looked very gay.

March 8. My husband went on board the Rochfort, with the girls[27] & Charles. He return'd much pleased with the ship, & everything belonging to her...

March 9. ...We have no less than 45 midshipmen on board & most of them very fine young men[28].

March 12. The Admiral & Capt. Green went to Pisa to dine with Adml. Sir William Hotham[29]. I took a walk with Harry & at three o'clock went to take a warm bath. The baths at S. Luca are really a beautiful building & uncommonly neat, all white marble, a marble pavement, much the nicest I have seen in Italy.

March 13. Lieut. Branford being on shore with the barge, we were tempted to go on board the Rochfort. The day was lovely & I was very much pleased with the ship. The quarterdeck is the largest I have seen. The guns being removed, the cabins will also be very comfortable...

March 16. The Admiral goes on board every day & is getting his cabin in famous order for us. We are to take up our residence on bd. next Monday.

March 19. The Admiral went on board to dine with the officers of the wardroom & slept in the ship...

March 20. It blew so hard that the Admiral could not return on shore today...

March 21. The gale continues, but my *marito* & the two boys came on shore at two o'clock. We shall remain here probably another week. Prince Metternich[30] is coming on Tues. & wishes to see the ship. The Emperor[31] will pay Rochfort a visit at Naples.

March 24. Mr. Branford came for me at six o'clock, & I got on board at seven. The cabins will be very comfortable, & I slept better than I expected in my cot & with the noise of washing decks etc. at daylight.

March 27. The morning was threatening & sea rather too rough for Prince Metternich to venture here. He went just out of the mole & his daughter[32] begg'd to go back... the Admiral proposes sailing tomorrow morning to Naples.

March 28. The ship got under weigh at nine o'clock, but there was so little wind that we were all day getting out of the channel of the Mellora Shoal, & were off Capraia & Elba in the evening...

March 29. We were off Corsica this morning & had a good view of the town of Bastia. The Corsican mountains were cover'd with snow. We have very little wind, but fair, & the weather quite lovely. Nothing can be pleasanter than sailing in this way, our band almost constantly playing on deck, a large party to dinner every day, & our cabin extremely comfortable.

March 30. We steal & slide along imperceptibly. We had rather more wind & clear of all land, the coast of Rome very distant. Maria, our Italian maid, exclaimed, *O Dio mio, quanto è grande il mare*! We had a little dance in the cabin this evening for the band & midshipmen to practise quadrilles & waltzes. Mrs. Munay & I were press'd in the service for a finishing English country dance.

March 31. We are getting on slowly, but nothing can be pleasanter, quite smooth water. We were in sight of Ponza this evening & if the breeze continues we shall get into the Bay of Naples tomorrow morning. I very much fear the Admiral will take us on to Malta[33].

April 2. ...The Admiral went on shore to look out for a house for us. He has nearly made up his mind to leaving us here while he goes to Malta. Sir Sidney Smith[34] & the Knights came on board & dined with us... Sir Sidney Smith was a most conspicuous figure. He had been to the King and came off in a shore boat, only two oars, with all his orders, four dingy stars and a round hat. He is looking old & talks much less than he did.

April 3. A great number of people of all descriptions come off to see the ship, & we had not anchor'd an hour yesterday ere Mr. Punch[35] came alongside, & a boat full of beggars...

April 4. I went on shore to church, the crowd of dirty, noisy people & horrible filthy beggars something quite disgusting. Really the church was more like a market place than a place of worship. The Consul lent me his carriage. I paid some visits, saw Ly. Sidney Smith[36], & the Miss Rumbolds, more affected & languishing than ever.

April 8. ...I went on shore to church & saw Sir Wm. Gill's house, which I think will suit us...[37]

April 9. We came on shore at ten & settled ourselves at Casa Ferrandino, which we have taken for three months, & are to pay 400 ducats for it. We have a great deal of room, & the windows are all down to the ground & look into a large garden or rather grove of orange trees, through which we have a walk to the Villa Reale, and from our bedrooms a very nice terrace, full of geraniums & flowers...

April 13. Capt. Spencer call'd immediately after our dinner to take the Adml. to wait on the Hereditary

Prince[38] & on Prince Leopold[39]. He came back quite ill & exhausted, having had to climb so many stairs that he almost fainted twice...[40]

April 16. I went with the girls this morng. to the Champ de Mars to see a cricket match, the shore against the ship. Our poor Rochforts were so beaten that they soon gave in, & played afterwards another match, taking one of the Mr. Knights on their side, which made it more even...

April 17. I went this morning early to the church of S. Giacomo for our Easter devotions. On my return met old Col. Paget with his niece, whose visit I luckily escaped. The poor old man is 86, & the French lady with him more than 60 - dress'd in a low, very low, gown, quite an object. He was Governor of Toulon when the English took it, & has since been in the service of the King of Naples.

April 25. ...I went with the girls this eveng. to the Dsse. de Narbonne's, terribly dull. They inhabit the house Sir Wm. Hamilton[41] had where I was married.

April 27. The Emperor arrived this morning, he was in an open German carriage with old Ferdinando, who had gone to meet him at Gaeta, & who held an umbrella for him...

May 1. The Duke of Ascoli[42] sent us from the King a very fine garland or plateau made of natural flowers for May Day. I did not know it was the custom here. The Dsse. of Narbonne gave a very pleasant ball this evening which was very well attended, & the girls danced a great deal. Prince Metternich has his daughter with him. She is married to Ct. Esterhazy, & is very much alter'd, not so pretty as she was, but more agreeable in her manners...

May 9. The S. Carlo open'd this evening & was brilliantly illuminated for the Emperor. A cantata was sung, in which there was scarcely any singing, but much dancing, & fine scenery introduced the different costumes of the Neapolitan dominions, a shower of sonnets on the occasion, festoons of laurel leaves & a fine & most ridiculous transparency[43], exhibiting the Emperor & King Ferdinando shaking hands. After the cantata we had the long ballet of *Orlando*...

May 16. ...In the evening we went to the opera. I was much delighted with the music of *Zoraide*[44], Rossini's *chef d'oeuvre*. Some parts are quite beautiful[45]. We stayed to the ballet of *Macbeth* & did not get home till near two.

May 17. The Emperor had intended going on bd. the Rochfort today at five, but at one o'clock sent to say he should not be able to do so. It is very vexatious, & the ship must go to Malta for provisions. The Admiral determined this morng. to sail next Mon., 24th, & to take us all with him, which is a great disappointment to me, as I was in hopes to remain here till the 8th July, having this comfortable house till then. We shall give it up to Capt. & Mrs. Noel, & to Malta go we must...

May 18. The Emperor, Empress, Archdss. Caroline with the King of Naples, Prince Leopold, the Prince & Princess of Saxony, & a numerous suite went at four o'clock this afternoon to visit the Rochfort. The barge & other boats met them at the mole, & Capt. Green steer'd the royal party. The admiral & Sir Wm. A'Court were on bd. to receive them. I went to Sir Henry Willoghby's lodgings at Sta. Lucia to see them off. It was a remarkably pretty sight from the multitude of boats that follow'd them. The Neapolitan ships in the mole mann'd yards & cheer'd as they pass'd. The Rochfort also mann'd yards & fir'd a double salute, on their going on board & on their leaving the ship, which they did at 6 o'clock in the King of Naples's boat, to go on board the Franklyn. They came on shore at sunset. A very unpleasant accident happen'd on bd. the American ship. Ct. Wurmbrand, the *Gd. Maître* to the Emperor, leaning against a windsail, fell down the after hatchway into the hole & broke his leg. Everything went off exceedingly well on bd. our ship & they express'd themselves much pleased. We dined late & went to the Fondo to see the *Matrimonio Segreto*[46], very pretty music of Cimarosa, but a little old & tedious. The ballet horrible. All the Court were there.

May 20. The Admiral, Capt. Green & I dined at the Margravine of Ansbach[47]. She was alone excepting Capt. Scarffe & Ct. de Préville, the latter a very sensible gentlemanlike man. She gave us a most excellent & comfortable dinner, but is a sort of woman that I look at with astonishment & a sort of horror... Several balloons went up this afternoon. In one was poor Mlle. Cécile & in the others & in the parachute they had sent up rabbits, who came down quite safe, but the poor girl had gone up too high, & was found in a state of insensibility when she fell, but soon recover'd. The *corso* was very numerous tonight. I think it dusty, noisy & unpleasant. We went this eveng. to the S. Carlo in the Duke of Leeds'[48] box. The music of *Elisabetta*[49] is quite beautiful.

May 23. I paid all my visits & found Ly. Sidney Smith pillow'd up, on a sopha with a blister on her side. She has just found out that the climate does not agree with her, & has prevailed on Sir Sidney to leave Naples as soon as our cutter can return to take them to Genoa... I call'd for the girls to take them to the opera. It was again Ricciardo & Zoraide, & the ballet of Macbeth, which I have got quite tired & was hiss'd this evening.

May 24. We got on board by four o'clock & left Capt. & Mrs. Noel in possession of our house...

May 25. We had got beyond Capri this morng. & had a very pleasant fair breeze all day, & Stromboli was in sight this evening at ten o'clock, fifty miles off... We have a very good French master on board for the youngsters. Cicey & her sisters are to take lessons. My cabin has been enlarged & is much improved by the stern gallery, which is made of iron, & so light it is scarcely susceptible.

May 26. We had a famous breeze all night & were off Stromboli before 6 in the morng. I got up to see it, but the top of the mountain was covered by clouds & I could not see the fire, but I am told it was very fine all night, & much more frequent & longer than the bursts of Vesuvius. Just now I could see four or five of these Lipari Islands, by twelve o'clock we got to the Faro of Messina, & went through the straits with a strong breeze... A pilot came on bd. to us, but we could have done as well without him. The passage is only two miles across, but Scylla & Charybdis[50] are not consider'd so dangerous as formerly. We had a good view of the town of Messina. The wind died away towards eveng. & we were becalmed off Etna, which is covered with snow, & has not thrown up any fire since 1812.

May 27. We were all day beating against a strong westerly wind to get beyond Cape Passero, the most southward point of Sicily. We had a good deal of motion & rolling about, but a firm, clear & pleasant day.

May 28, on board the Rochfort. I could not get any sleep all night owing to the motion of the ship & violent

20

noise on the poop just over my head. The wind continued foul but we were at anchor by one o'clock in the harbour of La Valletta. The island does not look at all inviting, the land being low & appears quite barren, but the entrance into harbour is one of the prettiest things I have seen. The ship sails into a narrow passage not half a mile across between the Castle of S. Angelo[51] & the batteries, which were crowded with people, & fired a salute as we passed, as did the other men-of-war, & was return'd by the Rochfort... The ship is anchored close to the shore, & the appearance of the buildings, being of a fine white stone, & very regular, makes the town look very handsome... We all went on shore at six o'clock. The Admiral was received by a guard & another salute was fired. We went first to the palace[52], which is a magnificent building... We took a drive to S. Antonio[53], the Governor's country house, & after drinking tea we returned to our ship.

May 29, on board the Rochfort. Sir Richard Plasket[54] & Capt. Maitland, who are living at the Palace, have been very civil in wishing us to remove there, but as we shall be here for a short time we prefer remaining on board, & everybody says the ship is cooler than the shore...

May 30. I went to mass & was much pleased with the church of St. John[55]. The pavement of marble & consisting of the monuments of the different knights who are buried there is the most beautiful thing I have ever seen. The Maltese women all wear black silk petticoats with a black silk scarf or mantilla over their heads, which I think is unbecoming & looks hot & fusty in this hot climate. We had a kicking horse to the *calesse* we have hired at a dollar a day & were obliged to walk part of the way. These carriages peculiar to Malta are very clumsy & uncomfortable. They are an old-fashion'd chariot body upon two clumsy heavy wheels, & shafts, with one horse, and the driver, accoutrè in the costume of the country with a red hanging cap, runs by the side of the horse, & I am told sometimes at the rate of seven miles an hour. I call'd on bd. the Revolutionnaire to see Mrs. Pellew, who has fitted up her cabin quite beautifully & is very comfortably settled. Her child was asleep, but seems a very fat fine boy. She makes as much fuss with him as most women do with their first child. We dined at the Palace... After dinner we drove again to S. Antonio. Nothing can be more horrible than the country. No verdure to be seen, as the island is all rock, & the stone is dug out, mould put in, in small enclosures, all wall'd in, & as not a sprig will grow beyond the height of the wall owing to the high winds & scirocco, the appearance of the whole island is uniform & hideous, stone walls & the dust quite intolerable. Still, the ground is highly cultivated & they get the two crops of corn a yr. The population is 40,000 inhabitants[56]. S. Antonio is four miles from La Valletta, the former country residence of the Gd. Master. The garden is very large & kept in excellent order by a Scotch gardener, but entirely wall'd in, & all the walks are paved with flat stone, there being no gravel or grass. We were shown a lioness & a famous farmyard...

May 31. ...I continue to have a multitude of visits, but the more I see of Malta the less I wish to live here, altho' a fat, vulgar lady of the dockyard establishment assured me there was excellent society & that she had lived fourteen years here. The weather is getting hot, but we are comfortable enough on board.

June 4, on board the Rochfort. We have a tiresome scirocco wind, with a disagreeable swell, which makes the ship roll about & very uncomfortable. A great deal of rain in the evening.

June 5. ...We took a walk on shore in the evening, but the country is so hideous & stoney & the head of this harbour marshy & offensive that it is quite disagreeable.

June 6. ...After mass I walked over to the church of St John, which is very fine & interesting, from the number of monuments there are to the Gd. Masters & Knights of the Order. All the different chapels are according to the different nations. The English had one. There is one fine painting, & the statue of St John christening our Saviour in the front of the church behind the great altar, by Cotonnier, is a very fine piece of sculpture[57]. We dined at the Palace & took our drive with Ly. Alvanley[58] & Capt. Maitland to S. Antonio, took a long walk in the gardens & returned rather tired.

June 8. We all dined today at Mr. Smith's the storekeeper, who celebrated his firstborn's christening & his wedding day. He has a small house in the dockyard & crowded sixteen people in a little stuffy room - the dinner endless, three courses & everything outré & quite out of character. Mrs. Smith is rather a pretty woman, affecting gentility. A few people came in the evening, & after an attempt at music, Mrs. Smith having performed on the harp & sung an Italian aria, an English country dance was set up & a supper ended the feast at ten o'clock. The bay where the dockyard is situated runs up a considerable distance, & from the houses on each side of it & a great number of boats which are moving about in all directions, gives it very much the appearance of some parts of Venice. Almost all the naval establishment is to be moved on this side of the water, & it was intended even the Admiral should have a house there, but my husband has applied for the old Admiral's House in Valletta[59], which he is to have & is a very excellent palace. I wish it was anywhere else than at Malta.

June 9. ...We took a drive in the eveng. & went to see Mrs. Whitmore's garden. It is laid out with much taste in one of the ditches of the town, with quantities of flowers. We afterwards went to Slima, the point beyond the quarantine harbour & reckoned one of the pretty drives. Sir Charles & Lady Pierson never missed one day during the three years they were here taking that conjugal drive together at two o'clock in one of the Maltese calisses - great constancy & perseverance - I should say amiability - on his part.

June 10. We went to St. John's Church at 9 o'clock, where the bishop sung High Mass, & there was a procession afterwards, this being Corpus Christi. The music was tolerably good. We went after church to the palace to see the Armoury Library & Sir Thos. Maitland's[60] collection of china, all very fine in their way. The armoury I was particularly struck with as it is arranged with much taste, & the armour of the Knights kept very clean & nice. It contains thirty thousand stands of arms... This was one of the hottest days we have had, with an oppressive scirocco, which has prevailed lately. There has been an eruption of Mount Etna, & the lava is now running for five miles. We took a row, *per prendere il fresco*, & the young ladies danced a quadrille on deck to cool themselves.

June 11, on board the Rochfort. I remained on board all day, & always find it infinitely cooler when I do not go on shore. The only way to stand this climate is to keep perfectly quiet. We are not to sail before the 21st.

June 15, on board the Rochfort. We are to sail next Mon., & every person in the ship seems to rejoice at going away from Malta... I went to La Valletta after dinner to some shops. It is the dullest place possible.

June 16. The Commissioner & Mrs. Woolley & Mr. & Mrs. Wilkinson dined with us. We took a row in the Commissioner's boat - the Maltese boat's crew terribly fusty.

June 18. I am quite tired of looking at the dead walls of Malta, & never stir out of my cabin except for a walk on deck in the evening.

June 21, on board the Rochfort. We got under weigh at daylight & even out of the harbour by seven o'clock. The Glasgow, Scout & Express schooner sail'd with us. We found a heavy sea & strong westerly breeze outside the bay, & had to lay to, almost two hours, waiting for our stupid Italian maid Maria, who had gone on shore, & almost lost her passage. The motion of the ship made poor Cicey very sick & the Admiral very nearly so. We got over to Cape Passero by one o'clock & found smooth water & a fair moderate breeze, which took us into the harbour of Syracuse just before dark, where we came to an anchor. The pratique boat came alongside, & we are threaten'd with 14 days' quarantine.

June 22, off Syracuse. I was delighted on first looking out this morning to see some trees & green fields along the shore, instead of odious white walls of Malta. The Consul came off to us, but we cannot obtain pratique under eleven days...

June 23, off Syracuse. We have a very good view of Mount Etna from this harbour, & at night it is particularly fine as the lava runs for ten miles, & even at this distance, about fifty miles, is very perceptible... The band played while we walked the deck & the girls waltzed.

June 24, Augusta. We sail'd at daylight & anchor'd at one o'clock in Augusta harbour, only 14 miles from Syracuse, but we had a foul wind to beat against. This is a very pretty bay, & there has not been an English ship of war here since the battle of Aboukir, when Sir J. Saumarez[61] came in here with six line-of-battle ships & six prizes. The entrance is rather difficult, & we came in first. The people came off to us & were very civil, but of course cannot give us pratique. We were allow'd to have a *guardiano*, & to land in the eveng. at the mouth of a small river, & our men drew their fishing nets, but did not get anything. The country is green, & full of olive trees. The town appears a poor miserable place. Their only trade consists of salt, but that is now very slack. The salt pits must make the shore rather unhealthy. The schooner sail'd back to Malta to get the letters by the packet, & I hope will bring Charles, who is coming in the Ganymede from Corfu.

June 25, Augusta. The Master is taking a survey of this harbour, having found the maps very incorrect, but I hope we shall sail tomorrow. We had a long row in the boat & attempted to go up a river, but got twice on shore & therefore gave up the attempt. The weather is very sultry & hot.

June 26, off Etna. We sailed at daylight from Augusta with very little wind & had it against us all day. We were off Etna in the evening, & the appearance of the mountain was the finest thing possible. The stream of lava must be very considerable, it is quite a torrent of fire & illuminates all the mountain. We could discern the crater very distinctly, & the bursts of fire from it were very frequent & very fine. It breaks out very near the summit of the mountain, which is still covered with snow. The Glasgow has parted company, having orders to go over

26

to Palermo, but was in sight all day. The brig remains terribly astern.

June 27, off Reggio. We had to beat all day against a foul wind, but had Etna in sight, & really it is the most magnificent sight just now. The black smoke which comes out of the crater is very thick, & is carried a considerable way like a black cloud. The scenery all day was quite beautiful as we sail'd close in shore from the Calabrian coast to that of Sicily, & I was looking out almost all day. We remain'd off Reggio, tacking backwards & forwards, between that place & Messina, not wishing to risk the straits at night with the wind against us. The Glasgow was not much before us, but poor Capt. Ramsden has not been even in sight all day.

June 28, off Milazzo. We beat through the straits at nine o'clock this morning. The scenery was beautiful. The Glasgow anchor'd last night off the Messina lighthouse, & was just before us. We had a fair breeze for Palermo but the Admiral put into Milazzo, where we anchor'd at seven o'clock. The point of Milazzo is cover'd with trees & there is a great deal of verdure, the whole coast being highly cultivated. The good people here have no power of giving us pratique, so we have no chance of getting on shore.

June 29, Milazzo Bay. A great number of people come in boats round the Rochfort to look at us. One mean-looking man in a miserable boat and dress'd in a nankeen, after talking to us some time, offer'd his services, saying he was *il marchese* so & so, & a set of girls in the next boat, dress'd more like housemaids then ladies, he introduced as his daughters. The whole of Sicily is now almost in a state of rebellion, as the government are enforcing the conscription which has not been attempted for 300 years. As married men do not enlist, there are nothing but marriages going on all over the country. It is reported that no less than 15,000 weddings have taken place within these few days, & some most ridiculous matches, old women of 80 to boys only 16; old men to girls of twelve years old. *Tous se marient*. It was dreadfully sultry & hot today, & the glass up to 80 in our cabin. The Admiral is making an alteration which will very much improve the cabins by taking off a window on each side & throwing the middle cabin all in one. The side cabins are large enough for sleeping rooms, & the whole arrangement is much more comfortable. The Scout only joined us this evening.

June 30, off Lipari Islands. We sat all day in Capt. Green's cabin, as ours are full of carpenters & workmen. The Admiral is delighted. Capt. Ramsden dined with us, & all got under weigh after dinner. He is going to Naples & we shall proceed to Palermo as fast as the wind will permit, but we had scarcely any all the evening & did not get round the Milazzo point.

July 3. A fair breeze at last brought us very prosperously into Palermo bay & by two o'clock we were at anchor. The mountains round this bay have a very wild & picturesque appearance, & the approach to Palermo & situation of the town are as pretty as that of Naples. Mount Pellegrino is a beautiful object. Capt. Maitland came on board. We had pratique yesterday & we were granted it immediately. The Admiral went on shore after dinner with the Consul, Mr. Lindemann, a German, a busy, civil & obliging person. Prince Landolina's house is quite ready for us, & the Princess sent a very civil message & her carriage to attend us, but I would not go on shore this evening. Ly. Alvanley has very small hot rooms at the Valentine Hotel.

July 4. I came on shore at ten o'clock & found Princess Landolina's carriage at the landing place. We went first to mass at the cathedral, & were desired by a fat *chanoine* to take off our bonnets, it not being the custom here to wear them in the church. We did so, but I think it would be more decent & respectful if these proper people kept the naked beggars out of the church. Some objects are quite disgusting. Boys & men with scarcely a rag to cover them, in a state of nudity, are allow'd to approach you, & one poor boy in a dropsy had his stomach quite bare, & really was a horrible indecent sight. We call'd after church for Princess Landolina, who came with us to the house which this Prince has been kind enough to lend us. It is more than a mile from the town, beyond the Marina Walk, rather small but fitted up quite in the English & French styles, & really quite a *bijou* - a verandah to the sea, with the sea breeze blowing right through the house, & a very pretty small garden at the back.

July 6. I went into the town & found it dreadfully hot & unpleasant shopping, but our villa much cooler than any other place. The glass on bd. was 84, in our drawing-room only 78, & the heat by no means oppressive as we have so much sea breeze... We have hired a Sicilian cook, who gives *les diners ā la mode du pays*, & tolerably good. I took a drive at the Corso, which is always very well attended, but spent the evening at home, enjoying *il fresco* in our garden & on the verandah, watching the fishing boats carrying large lights to attract the oysters, which have a pretty effect on the water, & looking at a comet which has made its appearance within these few days...[62]

July 9. The cutter arrived yesterday & brought letters. I was much pleased to hear that Ly. Burghersh[63] had been safely confined on the 18th June, & had a son...

July 10. I went this morning with Capt. Green, Harry & the girls to the Capuchin convent a mile out of the town to see the burying ground, where the bodies are preserved & hung about the walls or put up in niches - the most horrible & disgusting sight I ever beheld. Some of these bodies have been kept more than 200 years & are a most ghastly sight. In addition to these thousands of preserved dead, there was one poor monk laid out who had died in the morning & was at night to undergo the process of baking, & afterwards they are shut up in a niche for eight months ere they are exposed to view in these vaults, which are very extensive. Many of the Sicilian nobility are kept here in chests cover'd with velvet or red silk, and the key remains with the nearest relations, so that they come sometimes to visit these mutilated remains of their friends & relatives. These Capuchins are very poor & live on charity. There are 160 of them in this convent. We were not at all pleased with our visit. The smell is dreadful & the heat was excessive[64]. On our return we went to the manufactory of silks, which are very inferior to French & equally dear. They were painting very fine transparencies for the fêtes on the arrival of the Hereditary Prince, & the Frenchman who show'd them to us, explaining the subject of one representing Virtue, remarked that in this country *La vertu reste toujours sur la toile*. The cutter is gone on to Malta to carry an order from the Admiralty for the Ganymede to go home. The girls went with their father to the opera, & I remained *toute seule*, at home.

July 11. Mr. Fitzclarence[65] & Mr. Bannister dined with us. We went after dinner with Prince Pantelleria to see some races, & a national fête along the mole at the house of Princess Rasnaka, (?) a most civil & good-humoured fat lady. We came too late for the boat races, & she order'd another on purpose for me to see, which was very kind of her but scarcely worth having as the boats are very clumsy & get along very heavily. The horse races were still worse, but the concourse of people was very great, & the Sicilians seem a messy, noisy lot of people, almost savages. I drove to the Marina in the evening at ten o'clock to listen to the music, & took a few turns *à* la *Sicilienne.* I soon get terribly tired of this monotonous amusement, & prefer a good long drive or walk in the country.

July 13. We set out at one o'clock in the morning on our expedition to Mount Pellegrino... We found a large supply of donkeys at the foot of Mount Pellegrino, about two miles from the town, & left our carriages to mount our humble steeds. The road up the mountain, rather steep & rough, is not at all bad, but rather uninteresting. We had a fine moon to light us, & the night was particularly pleasant. The ascent is just four miles. A hermit lives about half way, lights up a little altar & asks alms of every passenger. We arrived rather sooner than we expected at the convent & church where the bones of Sta. Rosalia[66] were found. Monsr. Acuto had sent a multitude of cooks & servants with a letter to the *priori*, requesting he would allow us the use of a room for our *digiuni*, but the *signori canonici* were all gone to bed, & no knocking or persuasions would gain us admittance. Our Italian beaux were in a great rage, & call'd the ungallant priests all sorts of opprobrious names, but they merely shut the windows in our face & left us *à la belle étoile*. Our *digiuno* was laid out at the church doors on a table we procured from a neighbouring cottage, & we made the most ludicrous appearance, sitting down at break of day on the top of this bleak & barren mountain to a most elegant meal, consisting of everything which could have been procured at a ball in London. The finest linen, china, ice, fruit. In short, nothing was omitted, & as the day broke in the valley just before us, everything appeared to great advantage. We walked rather more than a mile to the top of the hill, where there is a small rotunda in brick, bearing the image of Santa Rosalia on the top, commanding a fine sea view, but not worth the rough & disagreeable walk we took to see it. On our return to the convent about six o'clock, we found the *chanoines* up, who very graciously came to invite us into the [?]. The Duca made bitter complaints for their rudeness, to which they made the best apology they could, & showed us the church, which is in the rock, consisting of a cave, where the bones of the saint were found. A marble statue is laid in it, richly dress'd, representing the young virgin Rosalia. Her bones are kept in a silver chest at the cathedral, & in gratitude of her having stopped the plague her bones are taken round the town once a year in a most huge & magnificent case, which is now preparing, & grand illuminations, fireworks & horse racing take place on the occasion. We did not find the sun troublesome until we reached the town, but found our drive to Romagnolo rather hot. We got home at nine o'clock & went to bed for a few hours to rest after our night excursion...

July 16. Mr. Oswald & Monsr. Acuto dined with us. The latter is a most civil & good-humoured person, his manners rather vulgar, & I believe was not very *noble*, but made his fortune in England by play, & keeps now a great establishment & everything *à l'anglaise*, except himself, for he is more like a cook than a gentleman. We went this evening to a party at the Prince of Trabia...[67] There was a great number of people there, but not one pretty woman, & I was quite amused at one fat merry-looking squat object who was dancing, & on inquiring her name was told she was the Marquesina, who was married at eleven years of age & has now three children. She is about seventeen. The party was more numerous than usual, & an attempt at a ball in honour of us, but I think we were a *gêne* to them & they seemed to prefer their blind man's buff & vulgar games...

July 17. ...most people seem to give up the fêtes as the Hereditary Prince has put off coming till August, & everything is to wait for him. We shall probably not stay for his arrival...

July 18. A fine westerly wind had made the weather much cooler & pleasanter, but we are sadly annoyed by the dust, which comes in clouds into our windows...

July 19. We have fixed our departure on Sun. next as it is in vain to wait for the fêtes. There is an idea that the Prince is afraid to come on account of the present discontented state of the island, & that perhaps the fêtes will not take place at all this year. This will only make the government more unpopular as the common people are so superstitious that they say Sta. Rosalia is very much dissatisfied & uneasy at this delay of her fête.

July 20. ... There was a violent scirocco for a few hours, which raised the glass in a moment to 96. Fortunately, it changed again towards sunset, & we were enabled to drive to Favorita[68], having procured an order to see it. This very small shooting villa of the King's is about five miles from Palermo at Colle, quite a little Chinese pagoda, remarkably small but rather neat & pretty. There is a quantity of game in the gardens & it stands prettily situated...

July 21. The morng. was so excessively sultry & hot that the Admiral would not venture on our little excursion. We set out at 2 o'clock in five carriages... The road is very fine & lined with aloes in full bloom, prickly pears & oleanders. The former is a formal & stiff plant & the bloom so ugly that I do not think it is worth being kept in a greenhouse as is the case in England. Bagheria is 8 miles from Palermo. All the Sicilian nobles have a villa here, & the situation is very fine between two bays and fine picturesque mountains... After dinner we went to see Prince Palagonia's[69] house. The present owner has taken away & destroyed all the monstrous & frightful figures the late Prince had had the odd fancy of collecting together. A few still remain in the courtyard... We also visited the Butera[70] villa, which is much the worse, & the wax figures in the cottage representing a convent of monks of La Trappe, a very miserable performance. The monks are in their dresses, & each in his separate cell. The Princess is now living at this cottage in the gardens of the Palace; it seems a very uncomfortable place & everything is very much out of repair & not kept up at all...

July 22. I went this evening to Monreale, rather a pretty drive, & fine situation on a hill, five miles from Palermo, but there is nothing to be seen except a cathedral which is now building. I went afterwards to the opera in Pss. Pantelleria's box.

July 25, on board the Rochfort. We got under weigh early this morning & sailed with a fair breeze towards Naples, the Glasgow, Scout, cutter & schooner in company with us.[71]

July 27, Bay of Naples. We came to anchor by six o'clock this morning & found the Capri & Neapolitan squadron still here. It is reported the Prince will not sail for some time yet...

July 28, Bay of Naples. The Admiral went to look out for a house, & with his usual good luck met with one which he has taken for a year for 1,000 ducats on the Chiaia[72]. I had several visits, Sir Sidney Smith who is applying for a passage to Genoa in the Glasgow, he is looking ill, old & out of spirits. Lady Smith is certainly in a bad state of health...

July 29, Bay of Naples. I went to see the house[73], Chiaia, & am very much pleased with it. The situation is excellent, being just beyond the end of the villa, good large rooms, with a small garden, & the whole house to ourselves, which is a great advantage... Sir Henry Willoughby, Mr. Browne & Mr. Procklington call'd after dinner. We took them on shore with us at 9 o'clock to go to the opera. I had Css. Nugent's box & I was much pleased with the performance; two ballets to please the old King who enjoyed a foolish naval fight, and only one act of *Zoraide*. S. Carlo is certainly a magnificent theatre.

August 1, Bay of Naples. After the *messa* at S. Ferdinando I went to see Sir Thos. Lawrence's pictures, & was much pleased with them. He has been doing the Pope's portrait & that of Cardinal Consalvi at Rome for the Prince Regent, also the Emperors of Russia & Germany, the King of Prussia's, & will now shortly return to England[73]. We met a great number of English there, & it was quite a lounge, & then paid some visits & return'd on board to dinner. I went in the evening to the S. Carlo in Ly. A'court's box to hear the Gazza Ladra[74]. A famous singer, Ambrosio, sings the base, but a most frightful woman acts the part of Pipo, la Pesaroni, in man's clothes & is an object, but a good singer. The ballet of *Hamlet* very dull & stupid.

August 4. ...In the evening we came on shore to take possession of our new house, which I found very comfortable. Our chairs, tables & sofas very much add to the appearance of it, & the view from the balconies is delightful. We have all the bay, Vesuvius, the villa & the coast of Posillipo. There was a *fête* of fireworks on the latter this evening, where the King went in his barge all illuminated. The effect was very pretty from our windows...

August 5. I am very happy to find myself on shore & settled in a good house for some time. We went on board to dinner. The Glasgow with the Sidney Smith tribe sailed this evening for Genoa...

August 7. ...We saw the Hereditary Prince & his family embark on the Capri for Palermo...

August 10. We dined at Gen. Nugent's at Resina, a fine country house he has between Portici & Favorita. The situation is very fine between the sea & Vesuvius, which rises from their lawn as if it belonged to their pleasure ground. There is a wood at the bottom of the mountain & he is cutting walks through it & improving it very much. The house is built on a layer of lava, & may any day be buried under it again. Capt. Webster & Sir Thos. Lawrence dined there.

August 11. Mde. Nugent lent me her box at the Fondo where I heard for the first time Mde. Garganelli in *Paul & Virginia*. The music is considered very pretty, by Guglielmi, but it is flat after Rossini's.

August 14. The weather very hot & glass up to 84. My husband much oppress'd by it & annoyed at going away...

August 15. The Rochfort was out of sight this morning...

August 17. We had a shower today, which I hope will refresh the air. The Neapolitans now expect cooler weather & call the 15th of August the beginning of winter, but the glass remains above 80 night & day...

Augusts 19. ...The opera house very brilliantly illuminated & the ladies in diamonds & Court *toilette*. A new opera, *Ercole*, a first attempt of a young Neapolitan composer, Morsadenti. Some parts were much applauded. The ballet of *Arsene* is also very pretty.

August 21. Augusta has not been well these two days with headache, which kept us at home both evenings.

August 22. ...Augusta took a drive & is better. The Corso more tedious than ever...

Sept. 3. Sir Richd. Hankey & Capt. Arden brought me the *Gazette*[75], giving the list of the brevet in the army & naval promotion, by which I see my husband is made a vice-admiral.

Sept. 4. ...We went to the opera this eveng. It closes on Tuesday for 19 days.

Sept. 5. I received a letter from my husband by which I find he was only five days on his passage to Toulon, & having received orders to join a French admiral at Pt. Mahon & to visit wit him the States of Barbary, he had sailed on the 22 Aug. on this service & did not expect to return here before the end of Nov...[76] Ly. Douglas lent me the key to her box. I went therefore again to the opera...

Sept. 8. ...We went this evening with Csse. Nugent to the opera, & much pleased with *Ginevra*. Certainly the music is much finer than Rossini's.

Sept. 9. The weather continues wet & unsettled & the *fête* cannot take place, which is a great disappointment to all the country people, who come from the mountains & from the islands in their finest clothes, bring provisions for one day & cannot afford to stay longer. Some of the costumes of the women are beautiful, cover'd with gold lace & very rich & expensive.

Sept. 10. A fine day was at last favourable to the *Fête*. All the ships came round to our bay & anchored in front of our house, dress'd up in all their colours, & looked very gay. All the troops filed off at one o'clock & lined the streets in a triple row, from the Palace to the church of Pie' di Grotta. They were all newly dress'd & very handsome. At ½ past four o'clock the guns of St. Elmo announced the King having left the Palace. The procession pass'd us & consisted of 14 carriages, all with six horses. The King's two state carriages had 8, the first empty, & the one he was in was the gayest thing I ever saw, a sheet of gold, quite bright, the top cover'd with blue velvet with white plumes, & the blue harness of the horses looked rather pretty. The ships fired three salutes. The number of people & troops made it a very gay & pretty sight.

Sept 11. I went early this morng. to the Convent of St Raphael... We were introduced in the convent & received by the nuns with much kindness. They allow'd us to hear mass & receive the communion from their grated tribune, & we found it very quiet & comfortable...

Sept.13. ...In the evening I went to a party at the Dsse. de Narbonne, not very gay, but all the world astonished at the appearance of a Baronne de Lepell, just newly arrived, the tallest & awkwardest still German figure I ever saw, quite a man in petticoats, poor thing. I quite pitied her. 'Tis said he married her for love.

Sept. 17. Psse. Jablonowska[77] did not receive, owing to the Archduke Leopold's wife having had a dead child. The poor thing, I hear, is miserable at having married her uncle, & was particularly unhappy at being with child on this account. She will think it a judgment of Heaven, & will have more remorse & scruples than ever. Princesses are very much to be pitied.

Sept. 19. In honour of the Feast of St Januarius the *lazzaroni* more noisy than ever from the moment it was daylight...

Sept. 20. The Spry sail'd into the bay to land some kangaroos for the King, a present from the Regent...

Sept. 24. The weather has changed so suddenly that it is quite unpleasantly cold & such a sharp cold wind the open carriage is scarcely bearable in the evening. I shall change my dinner hour to six o'clock.

Sept. 30. I received a letter from my husband of 11th Sept. at Algiers. They were to sail next day for Tunis. The Dey had refused to agree to their times, & if he perseveres in his obstinacy the Admiral says they must have a brush with him, which I shall not at all like. Csse. Nugent lent me the key to her box. I went, but was never more bored at any opera, *Ginevra* was horribly sung, & ballet *Il Flauto Magico* a stupid thing...

Oct. 1. Sophy Lushington came to spend the day with us. Ly. Lushington, Sir Henry & two eldest daughters are gone to Capri with Sir Henry Willoughby as only beau. He lives a great deal with them, but I believe they can make nothing of him, & the manoeuvre will not succeed in my opinion... I did not feel very well after dinner, & as I have not been quite stout lately, I preferr'd staying at home. I have been amusing myself reading Mlle. de Montpensier's[78] Memoires & all Miss Edgworth's[79] tales over again.

Oct. 4. A gala night at S. Carlo for the Hereditary Prince's name day, St. Francis. Csse. Nugent asked us to go into her box. We found her in her Court dress, resplendent with diamonds, but she was so unwell that she could not stay to see the new ballet, *Aladdin*, which did not please me much.

Oct. 5. ...The Admiral's letter was sent me this evening having been open'd & fumigated & came even without the envelope. He had suffered much from the heat, was to sail on the 1st for Tripoli & expected to be at Malta by the middle of this month. The Bey of Tunis gave as unfavourable an answer as the Dey of Algiers, & defies all the powers of Europe. The plague had been raging dreadfully, & my husband & the boys were locked up in a dirty house for 24 hours. He was very happy to get back to the ship.

Oct. 15. We went this evening to a ball given at Portici by the Duke of Noia[80], where 400 persons had been invited in the most wretched *casina*. A small courtyard was made into a temporary ballroom, where we were perished with cold, & the atmosphere in the rooms above was the other extreme of heat, quite an oven - the most ill-judged thing & worst *fête* I ever was at. We were home by 12 o'clock.

Oct. 18. The weather continues very bad. I went in the evening to the Fondo to hear an old opera of Weigl's, *L'Amor Marinaro*[81], some parts of the music rather pretty, & the *buffo's* acting good. Prince Leopold & his wife were there. *Elle n'est pas embellie par ses couches*[82]. The house almost empty.

40

Oct. 19. The weather worse than ever. It blows a strong gale of wind, & our house faces it. There is no keeping out wind or rain...

Oct. 22. A vile sirocco & thick fog, in spite of which I walked at the Strada Nuova...

Oct. 24. We had the two little Gages to dinner, & I went this evening with my three girls to the opera - a new one of Rossini, taken from *The Lady of the Lake*, but *La Donna del Lago*[83] is a very inferior performance and the worst music I have heard of Rossini, innumerable trumpets & only a repetition of his former operas, Pesaroni the only person that sung well, the others all more out of tune than ever...

Oct. 25. Mde. de Narbonne lent me her box, & I went early to hear the first part of the opera, which I had not heard yesterday. I liked it much better tonight, & it was very much applauded.

Oct. 29. The party at Psse. Jablonowska was rather full & pleasant this evening, but everybody being in Court mourning for the King of Sardinia, who abdicated some years back & died at Rome a Capuchin Friar,[84] makes the parties look sombre & dull, & we are to mourn two months.

Nov. 4, 5, 6. Spent three days at home, grumbling at the scirocco, which certainly makes one feel feverish, bilious, nervous, low & wretched. I was obliged to have recourse to calomel, & am better in consequence.

Nov. 7. We went to the opera this eveng., *Ginevra* very idly sung, but we had several visits in the box & found it pleasant.

Nov. 17. ...Ct. Préville[85] told me a large ship had been telegraphed[86] off Sicily, which I hope may be the Rochfort.

Nov. 18. Ly. Lushington lent me her box at the Fondo, where we heard *Ginevra* much better than at the S. Carlo.

Nov. 19. Sir Henry Lushington call'd on me immediately after breakfast to tell me the Rochfort had gone into Baia[87]. It was a very stormy bad day, but we drove towards Pozzuoli & met the Admiral driving towards Naples with Mr. Bingham, having got pratique as soon as he anchored, only five days from Malta. He is looking better than he did & a little fatter. We went this evening to Psse. Jablonowska, all the world there & very civil to us.

Nov. 21. Lush constant rain & bad weather. The cutter would not come round to land all the things the Admiral has brought...

Nov. 23. ...The cutter landed all our things, & my husband was busy putting down Turkey carpets, which make our rooms very comfortable indeed. He is to keep carpenters on shore to put the house in repair & secure the windows too.

Nov. 25. ...The Admiral fell fast asleep after dinner & could not be prevailed upon to go to the ball.

Dec. 7. We had only Capt. Green to dinner. The Admiral has a rheumatism, which prevents his sleeping & is very low & poorly.

Dec. 11. ...Sir John Burgoyne,[88] FitzClarence & Talbot came in the eveng. I found it terribly stupid. The Admiral having gone to the Fondo, & left Emma & I *toutes seules*, they amused themselves talking scandal & finding fault with every English girl in Italy.

Dec. 13. The Admiral & I dined at Sir Wm A'Court, a mixed party & half *literati*, rather boring. The Dss. of Marlborough[89] & her daughter[90], Sir Humphry & Ly. Davy...[91]

Dec. 16. We were all at home, & Capt. Green & I played at whist in the eveng. to keep the Admiral awake. His rheumatism is better & he has had good nights lately.

Dec. 18. (A third of a page is left blank.)

1820

Jan. 1. Since the sudden, awful & most heavy loss I sustained I have been involved in too much sorrow & misery to attempt giving any account of an event so calamitous in its consequences & for which I was so little prepared. A year which had begun with every prospect of happiness has ended with a misfortune which must weigh heavy upon me, but I must submit to the will of providence & bear my heavy affliction with Christian fortitude. I shall give as short an account as possible of these distressing moments. They can never be obliterated from my mind & are too painful to look back to. On Saturday, 18th Dec. my dearest & ever to be deplored husband was perfectly well, took his usual drive, & seemed in very good spirits at dinner. He took his nap after dinner, & Emma having a bad cold stayed at home, & he said he should stay also. I went to Psse. Jablonowska with Augusta & Capt. Green, & when I came home before twelve o'clock I found they had all gone to bed. Mr. Munro sent to me at daylight to say the Admiral was not well. I immediately went to him & found him complaining very much of the pain & palpitations at his heart, which he was subject to. He had been sick. His servant sat up with him all night & he had drunk a quantity of wine & water, above a bottle of white wine. I thought this had affected his head, for he talked in his sleep very incoherently, & we sent for Dr. Reily & also Dr. Griffith. Mr. Reilly bled him the moment he came, & this seemed to relieve his side & his breathing, but he remained in a state of stupor &

ruefully insensible. Griffith came at eleven, bled him again & called in Dr. Worth. Everything which art could suggest was done. He was put in a hot bath of rum & salt water, had three blisters applied, but, alas, nothing could save him, & he expired at ten o'clock without a groan or struggle - without a warning of his approaching end; & we are left to deplore his fate & the full weight of our loss. I was not with him at the dreadful moment. I did not apprehend any immediate danger, & the doctors wished me out of the way. I scarcely know how I bore the blow. Poor Charles was sent for, & arrived in the night. His feelings can be easily conceived. He had left his father quite well on Saturday & found him a corpse on Sunday night. The kindness I have experienced from all my friends is beyond anything that can be said, as also Capt. Green's & Mr. Munro's exertions & friendly behaviour. The King, who was much affected on hearing of this dreadful event, granted that the burial might take place with military honours, & Gen. Nugent came forward most handsomely on the occasion. The last duties were performed on Wed. 22, attended by all the officers, almost all the English here, cavalry & troops, and the Neapolitan marine, & followed by fifty carriages. The Duke of Leeds, Ld. Whitworth[92], Ld. Spencer[93], in short all the English were there & have shown the regard & respect they bore my departed husband. Sir Wm. A'Court sent an express to England; this will be a sad blow to Wm. Fremantle & poor Tom[94], who, I fear, will find himself in great difficulties at first. I do not know whether he has yet set out, & I shall not be able to determine what to do until I hear from England, but probably I shall remain at Naples till the summer. I have everything about me very comfortable & cannot bear to move. I could not see anybody until Wednesday the 29th, when I had a visit from Ly. Lushington, & the following days I saw Ly. Alvanley, Ct. & Csse. Nugent, the Dss. of Leeds & Mrs.

Pellew. The weather has continued horrid, incessant rain, & my poor girls cannot even walk out, & look wretched[95].

Jan. 6. ... Mr. W. Fremantle writes a good account of Stephen & Billy, but the state of the country is really most alarming...

Jan. 11. The Rochfort sailed into the bay. It was a dismal dark day, & the ship being painted all black made a miserable & wretched appearance[96].

Jan. 13. Capt. Green went to the King to return the Order of St. Ferdinand, lately in the possession of my dear husband...

Jan. 17. A continuation of rain & strong scirocco, which disagrees particularly with me. All my friends lend me books, which have proved a great resource.

Feb. 6. Cicey went to Albergo Reale with the Lushingtons to see the Corso, where the great fun is pelting with sugar plums. The poor children are so greedy to eat them that they get under the horses & carriages, & there was one poor boy run over & killed on the spot.

Feb. 7. I had a visit from the Dss. of Marlborough & Ly. Caroline, with their pet dog Chloe, the principal object of their care & affection.

Feb. 17. The Rochfort arrived at Baia early this morning & has been eight days from Malta. I shall go on bd. as soon as they are out of quarantine, probably next Monday... I wish I was off & still more that I was arrived. Wrote all my letters home.

Feb. 18 & 19. I went to see the studio. There are some fine pictures, but the most interesting thing is the collection of things found at Pompeii & Herculaneum, & the unrolling of the papyrus manuscripts. Sir H. Davy was there & explained to us the process.

Feb, 22. I went to see the Palace at Portici. It is very handsomely fitted up by Murat...

Feb. 23. The Rochfort came into the bay. Poor Capt. Forbes is dangerously ill of an inflammation in the bowels...

Feb. 24. Sent everything on board & we are to sail tomorrow... The account of the King's death arrived[97], & the Prince Regent was dangerously ill.

Feb. 25. I came on bd. at eleven o'clock. There was a great swell, which made me feel very uncomfortable & terribly nervous. Sir Henry Lushington was on board. We sailed about 4 o'clock with little wind, but found a strong breeze outside, & we were going between ten & eleven knots at night... Capt. Forbes was brought on bd. in his cot. He is out of danger. Much motion, everybody sick.

Feb. 26. A great deal of sea, the wind not fair, all the girls sick. I do not mind the motion & it got easier towards evening. The cabins are very comfortable, & Capt. Green has an excellent steward, & his table very well managed. We dine twelve persons every day.

Feb. 27. A delightful fine warm day & quite calm. A slight fair breeze in the afternoon. We have quite a party in the cabin every evening. Sir John Burgoyne is a wardroom passenger, & sleeps by choice in a hammock in the cable-tier with the midshipmen.

Feb. 28. We were 9 leagues from Cape Carbonara, the south-eastern point of Sardinia, in the morng., the wind scirocco, which would be a fair wind all the way to England, but there is too little of it.

Feb. 29. We came on very famously in the night, & were off the island of Toro at twelve o'clock, the wind east & quite fair in the evening.

March 1. A strong easterly wind. We went ten or twelve knots an hour all night & are come 204 miles since twelve o'clock yesterday. We are now about halfway to Gibraltar. We met the packet, & got some letters for Capt. Green, only 16 days from England. The Prince Regent, now George the Fourth, was nearly recovered & gone to Brighton[98]. A heavy swell in the eveng. & our fair wind all gone.

March 2. The ship very uneasy & a strong westerly wind, quite foul. Several heavy showers, but the weather cleared up at one, & I had a pleasant walk on deck. The islands of Cabrera & Minorca in sight.

March 3. A dreadful gale of wind from the north-west came on in the night & at two o'clock in the morng. carried away the main-yd. & shiver'd the mainsail to rags. The crash was tremendous, but luckily no accident happen'd. At daylight it blew most furiously, & owing to the loss of the yd. no sail could be set to steady the ship. I never felt so violent & unpleasant a motion, & could not get out of my cot till one o'clock, the confusion & comfortless state of the cabin quite ridiculous, everything gave way, & the waves dashed into the girls' cabin & they were not a little alarmed, but no one sick except Cicey a little. You could get nothing but a sea-pie for dinner, & the motion quite intolerable all day. Poor Mrs. Woolley kept her bed.

March 4. The gale continues & drives us back towards Sardinia - the carpenter at work night & day to repair the yard, & the forge could be kept at work today, tho' the rolling of the ship continues very heavy. But we got somehow dress'd for dinner, & sat at table with the chairs lashed all round. Emma has been sadly frightened, but is recovering her nerves. My cot came down in the night, & almost everybody else had the same disaster. The wind abated a little towards evening, but the swell is horrid.

March 5. We had some heavy squalls in the night, but the wind more moderate today, & we are steering west. I went upon deck, & never saw such a wreck as the poor ship - all the topmasts struck, & the quarter-deck having the appearance of a dockyd., nothing but the storm-sails set. Had we been on a lee shore, we could not have carried sail sufficient to clear it, & we were lucky to have plenty of sea-room. We dined more comfortably & played at loo, sitting on the deck. Poor Capt. Forbes very ill again.

March 6. No wind & our yds. & sails all put up. A little fair breeze from the eastward in the afternoon, & we are at last going the right way. We fell in with a Spanish brig, from Minorca to Tunis. They had been out a week, met the gale, & did not know where they had been driven to, but were steering quite wrong. The ship quite steady, & our cabin is getting comfortable again. The weather has been really dreadful, & one poor woman was nearly washed out of her hammock by a wave. The ship is so strained that it rains in everywhere.

March 7. 50 miles from Carthagena. A very fair breeze all night, & we are steering for Cape de Gatte, but the weather still squally, & constant showers of rain. We have felt it particularly cold.

March 8. We were off Cape de Gatte this morng. & 160 miles from Gibraltar. A most violent squall came on at eleven o'clock, & a most disagreeable sea. It blew for a few hours so violently from the eastward that we were under only one close-reefed sail, with the top yds. & quarter masts struck. The weather very threatening, & it rained all night, but the afternoon was fine, & the wind quite gone down, & we were becalmed off the coast of Spain, the mountains of Granada cover'd with snow, & the wind very cold indeed.

March 9. We had a fine easterly wind & sailed most delightfully all day about 9 knots an hour, but it looks dirty, & was too dark to venture running into Gibraltar tonight. We therefore shorten'd sail about 4 leagues off...

March 10. The wind shifted to the westward in the night & we were about 20 miles from Gibraltar, beating up with very heavy squalls. We were close in towards eveng., but gave up the attempt till tomorrow. Capt. Forbes is nearly recover'd, & all our passengers very good humour'd & pleasant. The Commissioner & his best half terribly annoyed at not getting into Gibraltar last night, quite a radical party!

March 11. I got up at six o'clock to see the Rock. The ship sailed in very famously with a fresh westerly wind, & we came to an anchor at ½ past 8 o'clock - the Rock very queer & in great beauty. Gen. Don[99] offer'd us his carriage, but it was too squally & bad for me to go on shore.

March 12. Gibraltar. It rained all night & early this morng., but it cleared after breakfast, & we went on shore at the Dockyard Gate, where the Lieut. Governor's carriage met us, a barouche & four with outrider & servant, a very gay set-out. We drove first to Mrs. Woolley's, & I was much delighted with the verdure & the beauty of the geranium hedges. Perhaps this is the most favourable time of the year to see Gibraltar, before the summer sun burns it & parches the ground. The Commissioner's house is really a delightful spot, & very much improved since I saw it, many years ago. We went to a small chapel to mass, where I understood part of a Spanish sermon. It was a very small place, & so crowded that the heat was quite oppressive. Mrs. Woolley gave us some famous luncheon, & afterwards drove with us to Europa Point. We saw the General's cottage, which is not worth seeing, walked to Monkey's Cave, & drove to the town to leave a card with Mrs. Don. We met the Governor riding, who is a fine-looking old man & like the late King. He was particularly civil to me. I return'd on board by 4 o'clock. A strong current & westerly breeze set in, which made the sea very disagreeable. Capt. Green dined on shore, but Capt. Forbes & Mr. Goring dined with us. Three American ships are here, but the Franklyn is gone to America. Several duels have been fought, & one very fine young man, a Mr. Smith, went out yesterday with an American officer, who behaved most infamously, having insulted him when he was on duty. The American fired three shots, each hit him, & it is feared Mr. Smith is very badly wounded.

March 13. Gibraltar. I went on shore this morning with the three girls & Capt. Forbes. Gen. Don sent us an open carriage he calls a caravan, a very awkward concern. We drove all round the Neutral Ground. There is a cordon drawn since the insurgents of Spain, who have taken possession of Cadiz, communicated with some place on the coast where the fury is still raging, & all intercourse with Spain is now quite cut off. The houses in the town are wretchedly small, & there is nothing worth seeing but the

Rock itself, & the Galleries & St. Michael's Cave. The weather has been so wet that I was afraid to visit them just now. We remained at Mrs. Woolley's till four o'clock. Her garden is quite enjoyable, but confined & overlooked. We had the same current & unpleasant sea to come off the ship, which makes me quite nervous & uncomfortable, & Mrs. Anderson was nearly upset in a small boat. Capt. Green dined on bd. with us, & expects to sail tomorrow as there is some appearance of the wind coming to the eastward. The American frigate & coaster sailed today. The officers of the Garrison sent them a general challenge & said they were ready to fight them, but at no greater distance than *two feet*. Upon this they got wisely under weigh. I am told some of these Americans practise firing at each other with cork.

March 15. The wind came round to the eastward at daylight, and we got under weigh... We had a very fair fine breeze to get through the Straits, & we pass'd quite a fleet of vessels, at least forty, who had been detained at the back of the Rock by the westerly wind. We were off the Cape of Trafalgar at dinner time, & about the height of Cadiz at night.

March 16. A very lovely day, but nearly calm at night, & we were close into Lagos Bay.

March 17. A fair breeze in the night, & we came round Cape St. Vincent & are steering north.

March 18. The weather continues lovely, a fair breeze at night, but almost calm in the day. We were 190 miles from Cape Finisterre at 12 o'clock.

March 19. We have a strong breeze from the north-east, which obliges us to steer to the westward - a very uneasy & uncomfortable sea.

March 20. A heavy sea. We are now in the Bay of Biscay, but obliged to steer north-west, which will take us to Newfoundland if the wind does not shift. It blows very fresh, & the ship has a great deal of uncomfortable motion.

March 21. A regular equinoctial gale, & really the ship is so uneasy it is impossible to have a moment's rest.

March 22. The first quarter of the moon, but little hopes of a fair wind. It has moderated a little. We are now in 15 longitude & 40 latitude, steering to the westward.

March 23. Luckily for us the wind shifted to the south-west, & we are going before the wind with a famous equinoctial gale, & rolling about most dreadfully.

March 24. The gale continues in our favour, & we run 245 miles in 24 hours, sometimes at the rate of 13 knots ½ in an hour. The motion dreadful. Impossible to sit in any comfort. We may be in the channel, & the Lizard lights are anxiously looked for as our dead reckoning & the lunar observation does not quite agree. Blowing hard at night, & going at the rate of 12 & 13 knots an hour.

March 25. We are still getting on with a strong northerly wind, but the master found himself out of his reckoning & considerably to the southward, drifting towards the islands of Jersey & Guernsey; luckily by carrying a heavy press of sail we made to Start Point & Bolt Head at four o'clock - smooth water in the eveng., the first comfortable day we have had, & sailing prosperously towards the Isle of Wight in the eveng.

March 26. We sailed into Spithead[100] with a fair wind...

# NOTES

[1] The escort provided for the illustrious Admiral Sir Thomas Fremantle and his family was doubtless a far cry from the one that the Countess of Blessington was to endure a few years later: 'At Velletri, the evening setting in, and a recent attack by banditti having occurred, we were advised to take a guard; nay, more than advised, for the master of the post alleged the positive necessity of the measure, and the postilions expressed their dread of proceeding without an escort. Though not a little loth, we at length consented to adopt the precaution; and a guard soon made its appearance, equipped and mounted in a style so irresistibly comic, that it was difficult to keep a serious face while looking at them. They looked as if by no means inclined to share in our hilarity; *au contraire*, they exhibited such evident marks of trepidation, that one of our party thought it advisable to hint to them that should the brigands make their appearance, and our guard not face them manfully, he would certainly fire on these last; a threat that seemed to alarm them not a little, as they saw that our gentlemen and servants were well armed... The wild and sallow countenances of the escort and postilions, formed a curious contrast with the plump, sleek, fresh-coloured faces of the English servants. The effects of malaria were as visible in the first, as were those of beef and beer in the second'. (*The Idler in Italy*).

[2] After the fall of Murat in 1815, the Kingdom of Naples become merged with that of Sicily to form the Kingdom of the Two Sicilies.

[3] This famous street was opened in 1536 by the Viceroy, Don Pedro de Toledo.

[4] Via Nardones should, strictly speaking, be called *Mardones*, this being the name of the Spanish grandee who owned houses here.

[5] Joachim Murat (1767-1815), Napoleon's brother-in-law, was King of Naples (1808-15). After Waterloo, with a price on his head, he went into hiding, then from Corsica conducted a foolhardy enterprise for the recovery of his kingdom, having refused Prince Metternich's offer of asylum. With a handful of followers he landed at Pizzo in Calabria, and on October 8th was captured. Summoned before a court martial, five days later he was executed.

[6] The husband of our diarist, Sir Thomas Fremantle (1765-1819), joined the navy as a twelve-year-old, and was one of Nelson's captains at the battles of Copenhagen (1801) and Trafalgar (1805). In 1810 he became an admiral. Our diarist calls him 'Fremantle' 'my husband' or 'the Admiral', never by his Christian name.

[7] Lavall Nugent (1777-1862), whom Lady Fremantle calls either 'Count Nugent' or 'General Nugent', was an Irishman who served in Sicily under Lord William Bentinck. In 1814 he was made a lieutenant-general in the Austrian army, and subsequently a field-marshall and a count of the Empire. He commanded the Neapolitan army, 1817-20, but was dismissed when King Ferdinand accepted the new constitution at the time of General Pepe's insurrection. In 1815 he married Giovanna, the only child and heiress of the Duke of Riario Sforza.

[8] It was Charles III of Bourbon who in 1737 provided Naples with an opera house that was worthy of this capital of music. Designed by Giovanni Medrano, a Sicilian architect, it was destroyed by fire in 1816 and immediately rebuilt. In 1765 Samuel Sharp had written: 'The Neapolitan quality rarely dine or sup with one another, and many of them hardly ever visit, but at the opera; on this account they seldom absent themselves, though the opera be played three nights successively, and it be the same opera, without any change, during ten or twelve weeks. It is customary for gentlemen to run about from box to box, betwixt the acts, and even in midst of the performance; but the ladies, after they are seated, never quit their box the whole evening' (*Letters from Italy*).

[9] The son of the Felton Hervey mentioned in note 11.

[10] Jérôme Bonaparte (1784-1860) was King of Westphalia (1807-13).

[11] Mrs. William Fremantle (1754-1850) was the wife of Sir Thomas Fremantle's younger brother after the death of her first husband, Felton Hervey.

[12] The crater of Agnano, flooded since the Middle Ages, was to be drained in 1866.

[13] Carbon dioxide.

[14] Precisely eleven? Maybe the guide had said 'una decina' (about ten) which Lady Fremantle misheard as 'undici' (eleven).

[15] Born in 1751, King Ferdinand IV of Naples and III of Sicily issued a decree dated 8th December, 1815, announcing that he had assumed the title of Ferdinand I of the Two Sicilies. He thereby ran the risk, according to an epigram of the day, 'by this joke of ending up at zero'. He died in 1825.

[16] In 1738 the royal palaces at Portici and Capodimonte were designed by the Sicilian architect, Giovanni Medrano, shortly after the completion of his San Carlo Opera House.

[17] On 12th March, 1817, Lady Fremantle wrote: 'We then went to see the *Sette Camere*, which are vaults, now in a garden, and was the reservoir of water for Titus's baths. We next visited the baths, and were shown some paintings which still are distinguishable in the ceilings, from which it is supposed Raphael took his designs for the Vatican. The French had a considerable part of these baths dug out, and a gallery discover'd and clear'd out, which had not been known before. We found it cold and damp, exploring these subterraneous vaults.'

[18] On 3rd March, 1766, Samuel Sharp wrote about Herculaneum: 'The antiquities found there are carried to the King's palace at Portici, and compose a most curious musaeum. I shall not give you a list of the ancient implements recovered from this city, but, amongst others, they have preserved the utensils of a Roman kitchen, such as gridirons, spits, pots, etc.' (*Letters from Italy*). It may be that the fame of this collection provoked the humorists of Velletri whom Goethe mentions (22nd February, 1787): 'As we arrived at the inn, some women, who were sitting before the doors of their houses, called out to us, and asked if we wished to buy any antiquities; and then, as we showed a pretty strong hankering after them, they brought us some old kettles, fire-tongs, and such like utensils, and were ready to die with laughing at having made fools of us. When we seemed a little put out, our guide assured us, to our comfort, that it was a customary joke, and that all strangers had to submit to it.' (*Italienische Reise*, in a translation by A.J.W. Morrison and Charles Nesbit)

[19] St. Januarius, Bishop of Benevento, was martyred at Pozzuoli c. 305. His blood generally liquefies at each of his three feasts.

[20] Cf. Théodore Vernes d'Arlandes: 'Some of the women shed tears of contrition and tenderness, and heave inflamed sighs. Easily distracted from their vehement yearnings, these relatives of St. Januarius resemble an interrupted actor who immediately resumed his tirade and the character of his rôle' (*Naples et les Napolitains*, 1859).

[21] Earl Temple (1797-1861), son of the first Duke of Buckingham, was to inherit this title in 1839. Their country seat at Stowe in Buckinghamshire, now a public school, lies within easy reach of the Fremantle house.

[22] Our diarist together with her husband and their children had rented the Palazzo Pucci since their arrival at Florence in August, 1818. This sumptuous edifice, the work of Paolo Falconieri and Bartolommeo Ammanati, was well known to them: they had already rented it from August, 1816, to February, 1817, paying 25 sequins per month. They found it comfortable, but they had to buy earthenware, linen, and two carpets.

[23] The future Admiral Sir Charles Fremantle (1800-69) was our diarist's second son; Stephen (1810-60) the fifth.

[24] Permission to disembark after quarantine or after producing health certificates.

[25] Henry Fremantle (1802-20) was our diarist's third son.

[26] Henry Monroe was secretary to Admiral Sir Thomas Fremantle.

[27] Our diarist's daughters were Emma, Augusta and Cecilia (Cicey).

[28] It is more than likely that this judgment included an element of snobbery: Sir Thomas had already written to his brother William: 'I hope they [the Admiralty] will send me gentlemen at least, I dread having a lot of ill-looking fellows.' He preferred the sons of the aristocracy, who entered the service as a result of patronage, to boys nominated by the Admiralty.

[29] Sir William Hotham (1772-1848) had served with Nelson in Corsica. He was the son of General Hotham, whose brother, Lord Hotham, was commander-in-chief of the Mediterranean Fleet when Captains Nelson and Fremantle distinguished themselves in an action against the French.

[30] Klemens, Fürst von Metternich (1773-1859), the most resolute champion of conservative principles in his day, was a protagonist in the struggle against Napoleon, and advanced Austria to the front rank amidst European powers. His appearance in Naples provided grave suspicion. Some even went so far as to say he had urged Luigi de' Medici, the King's counsellor, to provoke disorders so that Austria might have a pretext for interfering in the politics of the Two Sicilies.

[31] Franz I, son of Leopold (Grand Duke of Tuscany and subsequently Holy Roman Emperor) was the first Emperor of Austria. Born at Florence in 1768, he died at Vienna in 1835. We encounter him when he came back to his native country after an absence of thirty years. The visit was a purely political one.

[32] Maria, Gräfin Esterhazy (1797-1820) inherited her mother's weak lungs. Metternich, who loved her more than any other woman, called her his companion, friend and better self.

[33] Malta was a British possession from 1815 to 1964 and the Royal Navy's principal base in the Mediterranean.

[34] Sir Sidney Smith (1764-1840), a naval officer who, vain as he was brilliant, in the heroic defence of Acre (1799) was the first to defeat Bonaparte on land. In 1806, calling himself King Ferdinand's commander-in-chief, he disseminated a proclamation through Southern Italy, exhorting the insurgents to join forces with his sailors and marines. In 1812 he was in the Mediterranean as second-in-command to Admiral Sir Edward Pellew, later Lord Exmouth.

[35] 'Punch' is an abbreviation of 'Punchinello', which derives from the Italian *pulcinella*. However, J.B.S. Morritt in a letter from Naples, dated 17th November, 1795, writes: 'I have observed that there are very few traits of an English Punch in an Italian Polcinello, who really is a very witty and excellent buffoon, and certainly outshines plain Punch in every respect.'

[36] Caroline Smith, before she married Sir Sidney, was the wife of Sir George Berriman Rumbold.

[37] On April 12th Sir Thomas wrote to his brother William: 'On my arrival here my first business was to find a house to settle my family in, and I bustled about in damp rooms by which means I caught a severe cold.'

[38] The Crown Prince, husband of his cousin Maria Clementina, who was the daughter of the Emperor Leopold II, was to succeed to the throne of the Two Sicilies as Francis I (1825-30).

[39] Prince Leopold (1790-1851), sixth child of King Ferdinand, married his niece, sixth daughter of the Emperor Francis I.

[40] Sir Thomas Fremantle was permanently weakened by the arm wound he received in 1797.

[41] Sir William Hamilton (1730-1803) was British Minister to the Court of Naples during the last 36 years of the 18th century. He embellished the Palazzo Sessa with his collection of antiquities and modern art, and from 1791 with Emma, his second wife, who gave Nelson a daughter in 1801. In that year our diarist wrote: 'Lady Nelson is suing for a separate maintenance. I have no patience with her husband, at his age [forty-two] and such a cripple to play the fool with Lady Hamilton.'

[42] Troiano Marulli, Duke of Ascoli, was the King's mentor and Commissioner of Police.

[43] Transparencies, *i.e.*, pictures illuminated from behind, were very popular at this time, and were applied not only in the theatre but also to window blinds, and, with varnish, even to prints. In *An Essay on Transparent Prints and on Transparencies in General* (1807), Edward Orme wrote: The art of painting transparencies on linen, silk, and gauze, with oil colours, has been known in Asia from time immemorial, and long practised in Europe.' He added that for large works 'distemper or body colours should be used, mixed up in quantities. Or you may paint upon the same ground with oil colours, occasionally diluting with spirit of turpentine; and you may likewise mix with them some of the transparent varnish.'

[44] *Ricciardo e Zoraide* (1818), an opera by Gioacchino Rossini (1792-1868).

[45] The word 'quite' means utterly. It will be observed that Lady Fremantle's opinions tend towards one extreme or the other. This

doubtless tells us something about her character, but it is also typical of her era. In *Histoire de la Peinture en Italie* (1817), Stendhal observes: 'Everything is *execrable* or *divine*, and when people grow tired of one of these words for an object they adopt another.' But the language of these diaries is unquestionably dictated by the heart, far removed from the affectations of society.

[46] *Il Matrimonio Segreto* (1792) is the most celebrated opera by Domenico Cimarosa (1749-1801). It is based on *The Clandestine Marriage* (1766), a comedy by George Colman the elder (1732-94), who was born in Florence where his father was accredited as British Minister Plenipotentiary, and by David Garrick (1717-79), the great actor. The plot was suggested by William Hogarth's series of paintings called *Marriage à la Mode* (1743-45), which is now in the National Gallery, London.

[47] The Margravine of Anspach was formerly Lady Craven.

[48] George, sixth Duke of Leeds (1775-1836), was one of the Tories who, with Wellington, were to change their minds on the question of Catholic Emancipation, thus paving the way for the act of 1829.

[49] *Elisabetta, Regina d'Inghilterra*, an opera by Rossini (1815), was based on *The Recess, or a Tale of other Times* by Sophia Lee (1750-1824), one of the earliest historical novels in the English language (1785).

[50] Scylla is a district in the province of Reggio Calabria. The rock of this name projects some 30 yards into the sea. Charybdis is a whirlpool mentioned in the *Odyssey* (XII, 103ff) and situated opposite Scylla off the Sicilian coast. Also in the myth of the Argonauts recurs the name of this whirlpool, which Jason and his followers managed to survive, thanks to the help of Thetis. When the wanderings of Ulysses were localized in the West, perhaps in consequence of the voyages of the Chalcidians in these waters, Charybdis too was placed in the Strait of Messina, where it was identified with one of the many turbulences caused by the clash of currents. From the pen of Mark Twain not even Scylla and Charybdis managed to escape, as is clear from this passage in *The Innocents Abroad* (1869): 'The city of Messina, milk-white, and starred and spangled all over with gaslights, was a fairy spectacle. A great party of us were on deck smoking and making a noise, and waiting to see famous Scylla and Charybdis... One of the boys said:

"Hello, doctor, what are you doing up here at this time of night? - What do you want to see this place for?"

"What do I want to see this place for? Young man, little do you know me, or you wouldn't ask such a question. I wish to see all the places that's mentioned in the Bible."

"Stuff - this place isn't mentioned in the Bible."

"It ain't mentioned in the Bible! - *this* place ain't - well now, what place is this, since you know so much about it?"

"Why, it's Scylla and Charybdis."

"Scylla and Cha - confound it, I thought is was Sodom and Gomorrah."

[51] On its acropolis, the site of a temple of Juno, Fort Sant' Angelo rises at the seaward end of Birgu. It was the Magisterial Palace until the Knights moved to Valletta after the Great Siege of 1565.

[52] The Magisterial Palace at Valletta was designed by Gerolamo Cassar in 1571. Patrick Brydone in *A Tour through Sicily and Malta* (1773) remarked that the Grand Master of the Knights of Malta was more commodiously housed than any other sovereign in Europe, save, perhaps, the King of Sardinia. In 1800 this impressive building became the seat of the British Governor.

[53] The British Governor lived in this former country residence of the Grand Master, the Magisterial Palace now being confined to administrative use.

[54] Secretary to the Governor of Malta.

[55] The Conventual Church of the Knights of Malta at Valletta was begun in 1573 to the designs of Gerolamo Cassar. The Baptist is patron saint of the Order.

[56] Less stringent are William Young's observations in his *Journal of a Summer's Excursion* (1772): 'Malta is about sixty miles in circuit; a mere rock, in many parts absolutely bare, in others covered with a foot and an half of very rich mould; a great deal of which hath been brought from Sicily, and of which the proprietors are extremely tenacious; walling their several possessions into small squares, to prevent the earth being washed away by a heavy main, into their neighbour's territory; so that the country from an eminence, has the appearance of a large chess-board. The whole island is a fine example of what industry can draw from an ungrateful soil; every spot is occupied; the whole is a rich picture of villages, pleasure-houses, and gardens.' In *Guida dell' isola di Malta* (c. 1835) J. Quintana writes: 'The soil of Malta, though rocky, is rendered so fertile by the industry and application of the Maltese peasant that everything which is offered for sale in our markets has been produced on the island. Foreigners are amazed by this.'

[57] This marble group, which stands in the recess of the fasle apse and provides the church with its focal point, is by Giuseppe Mazzuoli (1644-1725), not by 'Cotonnier', as Lady Fremantle says. However, the brothers Nicolas and Raphael Cotoner, successively Grand Masters whose reigns stretched from 1660 to 1680, commissioned it. As for the 'fine painting', this is probably the altarpiece by Mattia Preti, who was known as il Cavalier Calabrese (1613-99), in the Chapel of St. Catherine, which belongs to the

Italian langue. It is unlikely that her Ladyship would have found much to admire in *The Beheading of St. John the Baptist*, which was then hung in the Chapel of the Most Holy Crucifix.

[58] Anne, Lady Alvanley was the widow of the first Lord Alvanley (1744-1804), a lawyer and politician.

[59] The sixteenth-century Palazzo Raimondo in South Street was, as 'Admiralty House', the residence of the commander-in-chief of the British fleet in the Mediterranean from 1821 till 1961, when it was rebuilt, and since 1974 is the National Museum of Fine Arts.

[60] Sir Thomas Maitland (1759?-1824) became the first British Governor of Malta during the plague of 1813 and immediately imposed a drastic quarantine. A fervent reformer, he resorted to an absolutism which gained him the nickname of 'King Tom'.

[61] Sir James Saumarez (1757-1836), a native of Jersey, was Nelson's senior captain at the Battle of Aboukir (1798).

[62] Discovered by Tralles, '1819 II' was one of the Great Comets of the 19th Century. It appeared from July 1st till October 25th.

[63] Priscilla, daughter of the third Earl of Mornington, married in 1811 Lord Burghersh (1784-1859), who during the years 1806-7 was Vice-Adjutant-General in Sicily and Egypt. He served in the Peninsula War and the French campaign. In 1815 he became a Knight Grand Cross of St Ferdinand and Merit and went to Florence as Minister Plenipotentiary of Parma, Lucca and Modena, besides Florence itself. He was a general in the Crimean War. In spite of his military and diplomatic eminence, Lord Burghersh is principally remembered as the first President of the Royal Academy of Music, which he founded in 1822. Here over a period of thirty-seven years he controlled the concert programmes. Like many aristocrats, he considered Italy to be the sole source of music, and insisted on Italian opera to the exclusion of all other music, with the sole exception of his own compositions. These, remarkable more for their existence than their quality, are in an outdated Italian style, lacking in originality. But the respect that was shown for his social rank helped raise the status of the musical profession in Great Britain.

[64] Lady Fremantle's reaction is typical. Among the few travellers who have something positive to say about these corpses is Dominique Fernandez, the author of *Mère Méditerranée* (1965): 'At any rate, in death they are not alone, and, if they have lost their colours, they are in company still... To be together! To experience the magic of contact! Are they not happy to have escaped the seclusion of the tomb? Are they not happy to have been spared what they fear most in the world, whether this one or the next: solitude? As for the lugubrious light and the white silence, these, after all, are of little importance: they are elbow to elbow.'

65 One of the illegitimate sons of that Duke of Clarence who served with young Captain Nelson and became King William IV (1830-37).

66 According to legend, St. Rosalia was born at Palermo, the daughter of Sinibaldo, the seigneur of Rose and Quisquina and a kinsman of William I, King of Sicily. Wonderfully beautiful, she soon ceased to take any care of her looks and led a life of penitence in a grotto in Quisquina and then in another on Monte Pellegrino, outside Palermo, where she died on 4th September, 1160. No trace could be discovered of either her body or her lodging. In 1625, however, while a plague was raging, Rosalia appeared on Monte Pellegrino to a soap-maker, to whom she revealed that in such and such a grotto her bones had been lying for nearly five centuries, and that if these were taken to Palermo they would put an end to the affliction. The bones were discovered, and once this sacred body had been verified it was transported with great pomp. Diarists and historians declare that, wherever the revered remains passed, there was a guarantee of cure; in a single day Palermo was saved. Lampedusa's *The Leopard* reveals that Father Pirrone, in 1861, had to undergo 'nausea at seeing patriotic pictures painted on carts and these culminated in the rhetorical scene of a flame-coloured Garibaldi arm-in-arm with a sea-blue St. Rosalia.'

67 Giuseppe Lanza, Prince of Trabia (1780-1855), succeeded Luigi de' Medici as Finance Minister.

68 This royal estate, as Ferdinando Mondini says in an article entitled *A "La Favorita": Il Lungo Esilio dei Borboni di Napoli*, 'offered, like the one at Portici, which possessed the famous cabinet of Capodimonte porcelain with Chinese decorations, the double attraction of fishing and the chase.' Designed by Venanzio Marvuglia in 1799, this extravaganza was influenced by Sir William Chambers (1723-96), the architect of the pagoda at Kew and author of *Designs of Chinese Buildings* (1757), in which he writes: 'I look upon them as toys in architecture.' Chambers also influenced the Royal Pavilion at Brighton and Sans Souci at Potsdam.

69 This villa is the creation of Francesco Gravina, Prince of Palagonia, whose grandson lived in rooms that were decorated with bizarre taste, including a hall covered in mirrors at strange angles, and he adorned the garden wall with 62 grotesque statues. The denigration that these underwent from the pen of Lady Fremantle was typical until the arrival of the surrealists. However, Leon Battista Alberti (1404-72) had already said in his *Ten Books of Architecture*: 'Between a house in town and a house in the country, there is the difference that the ornaments for that in town ought to be much more grave than those for a house in the country, where all the gayest and most licentious embellishments are allowable.'

[70] Villa Butera is called the Charterhouse on account of these figures of historical characters dressed as Carthusian monks.

[71] On 25th July Sir Thomas Fremantle wrote to his brother William: 'Our last voyage has been quite delightful, we were 3 days off Etna which was blazing to a degree you can form no idea, the lava running 10 miles, at night it was quite beautiful and in the course of 3 weeks we have seen Vesuvius, Stromboli and Etna all in flames, nothing is to be compared to the latter.'

[72] 'Chiaia' is a corruption of *playa*, which is already to be found in the letters of St. Gregory, and it was the name of the whole of the western coast of Naples. De Falco wrote: 'I shall go for a stroll along the lovely, sunny, graceful coast that we call *Chiaia*, just as by corruption they pronounce "più" *chiù*, "piove" *chiove*, "pianello" *chianello*, etc.'

[73] The Prince Regent, who from 1820 to 1830 was to reign as George IV, commissioned Sir Thomas Lawrence (1769-1830) to paint portraits of all the most prominent personages in the struggle against Napoleon. The portraits adorn the walls of the Waterloo Chamber at Windsor Castle.

[74] An opera by Rossini (1817).

[75] The word 'Gazette' comes from the Italian *gazzetta*, a coin that gave its name to a sixteenth-century Venetian newspaper. *The Oxford Gazette* was founded in 1665, and under the name of *The London Gazette* (or simple *The Gazette*) became the register of official appointments.

[76] The pirates of the Barbary States were ultimately suppressed when Spain and France occupied a large part of North Africa. Meantime in 1818 the Congress of Aix-la-Chapelle charged Britain and France with the delivery of an ultimatum to the Beys of Tunis and Tripoli and the Dey of Algiers. Consequently these potentates who had dared defy the European powers received a visit from Admirals Sir Thomas Fremantle and Jurien de la Gravière, to whom they made some empty promises.

[77] Wife of Prince Ludwik Jablonowska (1784-1864), Austrian Minister in Naples.

[78] Mlle de Montpensier, known as 'la Grande Mademoiselle' (1627-93), was the daughter of Gaston d'Orléans, brother of Louis XIII.

[79] Maria Edgeworth (1767-1849) was a novelist and short-story writer whose themes were Irish life and children.

[80] Giovanni Carafa, Duke of Noia, founded a museum of antiquities.

[81] *L'Amor Marinaro ossia Il Corsaro de Gamberra* (1797), opera by Joseph Weigl (1766-1846).

[82] Childbirth has not improved her looks.

<sup>83</sup> *The Lady of the Lake* (1810) is a poem by Sir Walter Scott (1771-1832). *La Donna del Lago* was performed for the first time on September 4th, 1819.

<sup>84</sup> Carlo Emanuele IV (1751-1819) reigned from 1796 to 1802, when he abdicated in favour of his brother Vittorio Emanuele and joined the Jesuits in Rome.

<sup>85</sup> A French refugee, Count Préville became the High Admiral of the Two Sicilies.

<sup>86</sup> At that time, needless to say, telegraph was optical, i.e. semaphore.

<sup>87</sup> On December 6th Sir Thomas Fremantle wrote to his brother William: "You can't imagine how snug the ship lies at Baia, Naples Bay is too open, with much sea in the winter, I should not have ventured to keep the squadron there, but in the summer season".

<sup>88</sup> Sir John Burgoyne (1782-1871), a sapper, saw service in the Peninsula War, the War of 1812 and the Crimean War.

<sup>89</sup> Susan, Duchess of Marlborough (1767-1841), wife of the fifth duke, who in 1801 was tried for crim. con. with Lady Mary Anne Sturt, wife of Charles Sturt. A great bibliophile, in 1812 the duke bought a copy of the *Decameron*, printed by Valdarfer (1471), for £2,260, an event which led to the creation of the Roxburghe Club, of which he was a founder member. In 1819 he sold the *Decameron* to Earl Spencer for 875 Guineas (£919). In his last years 'he lived in utter retirement at one corner of his magnificent palace, a melancholy instance of the results of extravagance' (*Annual Register*, 1840). He is the subject of a biography, *The Profligate Duke*, by Mary Soames, a descendant of his and a daughter of Sir Winston Churchill.

<sup>90</sup> Lady Caroline Spencer-Churchill (1798-1824) in 1822 married David Pennant and died three weeks after having given birth to a daughter.

<sup>91</sup> Sir Humphry Davy (1778-1829), chemist, is considered the founder of electrochemistry. He demonstrated that chlorine was a simple substance. He also invented the miners' safety lamp. Such was his international fame that in 1813, during the war, he travelled on the Continent with the permission of Napoleon. While in Italy he performed experiments on torpedoes, and worked in the laboratory of the Accademia del Cimento on the combustion of diamonds. At Pavia he met Count Alessandro Volta before returning to England. On 26th June, 1818, he again set foot on the Continent and made his way to Naples with the aim of unrolling and rendering legible the ancient papiri. He suggested various measures, including the application of hot air, but with limited success.

<sup>92</sup> Earl Whitworth (1752-1825) had been a lord since 1800, when a large number of peers were created to effect the union of Great

Britain and Ireland. These, as a condition of their ennoblement, were required to support the Government with their votes in the House of Lords and with their influence in the House of Commons. In *Last Journals*, Horace Walpole called them 'a mob of nobility' and added that 'the King in private laughed much at the eagerness for such insignificant honours.'

[93] The 2nd Earl Spencer (1758-1834) was First Lord of the Admiralty, 1794-1801. His historical importance lies chiefly in the high regard he had for Nelson's qualities.

[94] Thomas Francis Fremantle (1798-1890), politician, was our diarist's firstborn. In 1821 he was made a baronet in recognition of his late father's services, and in 1874 he was raised on his own account to a barony, with the title of Cottesloe. In our own day one of the houses of the National Theatre was named after the fourth lord.

[95] Henry Monroe, secretary to Sir Thomas, wrote to William, the brother of the deceased: 'Lady Fremantle and the ladies [her daughters] are in a state not to be described. Her Ladyship tries to bear with fortitude, but suffers much. Charles did not see his father die, he is now here, and his grief is agonizing.'

[96] The Rochfort also bore its yards crossed diagonally as an additional sign of mourning.

[97] The reign of George III (1760-1820) was the longest of any British sovereign till that of Queen Victoria (1837-1901).

[98] Brighton, a seaside resort on the English Channel, owed its exceptional elegance to the frequent presence of the Prince Regent.

[99] Sir George Don (1754-1832) was Lieutenant-Governor of Gibraltar.

[100] Off Portsmouth.